The Imaginary Emperor

A Tale

by

Steve Bartholomew

The Imaginary Emperor
By Steve Bartholomew

Published 2011 by Dark Gopher Books
ISBN 10: 0615488854
ISBN 13: 978-0615488851

http://www.untreedreads.com

Dear Reader:

Please do not charge the author of this yarn with historical inaccuracy. He freely admits to it. This narrative is an appreciation, not a history. There really lived an Emperor Joshua Norton, who inspired, among other things, this story. We know the bare outline of his biography, his dates of birth and death, his published proclamations and so on. What we do not know are his innermost thoughts and feelings, what people he talked to, the sort of things he did in private when no one was looking—whether he was sane or mad. Did he really have a secret hoarded treasure? Perhaps.

In fact, many articles in print about Norton are scurrilous and full of inaccuracies. For example, some folks still think that he owned those two valiant canines, Lazarus and Bummer. In reality, he hated the mangy curs. One could go on and on, but we won't. The author is interested not so much in the bare facts of the Emperor's life, as in his spirit.

The author hopes the reader will find some fun in reading this tale. If one prefers facts, or what passes for facts, please pick up an official history book.

Part I

Chapter 1

The two men with their seconds meet at dawn. The sky as usual is overcast, with a faint drizzle which is not rain but merely a heavier kind of fog. Out here at Lake Merced, just outside the city limits, the men can hear the distant booming of surf. Only a low hill separates them from the sea.

The seconds of the two men meet and confer. Apologies are offered and refused. One of the two principals, the challenged, looks about with great care, knowing within himself it will be his final look at the world. His last name is Bradley. Oddly, both men have the same first name, William. Bradley never looks at his opponent, who had once been his friend. Bradley's mind is empty, thinking of nothing, least of all the long chain of events which has brought him here. He tries to fill his head with a sight of the lake, the trees, the sound of surf that comes from over the hill.

A coin is tossed. The challenger, whose last name is Perry, wins the toss. This gives him choice of weapons. Later, it will be whispered the coin toss was a cheat, but this is never proved. Perry brings forth a pair of Belgian .58 caliber dueling pistols. He has been practicing with these weapons all week. They both have hair triggers. Later, his second will claim he informed Bradley's second of this fact. He in turn will deny that.

Now Perry gets choice of position. He stands with his back to the sun, which struggles to break through the mist. Bradley stands a measured distance away. One of the seconds begins a long count of three. One, two…Bradley raises his weapon. With his finger barely touching the trigger, it discharges into the ground. He drops his arm and stands still, waiting for Perry's shot.

Perry is a marksman. He takes his time, aims and fires. The bullet strikes Bradley in the side. He does not fall, but is led from the field.

"Only winged the bastard," Perry mutters. Three days later, Bradley is dead.

* * *

The young reporter lifted his pencil from the notepad on which he had been scribbling. He was using a form of shorthand, which he had learned at school in St Louis, and of which he was quite proud. He could also use a typewriter. He felt he was qualified for a better assignment than the one he was on now. But then, what could he do? Feature story, they called this. Maybe if he turned in something halfway interesting for the Sunday supplement, he might get a try-out on the crime desk, which was where he wanted to go.

He said, "But Judge Buxby—why did you tell me that story? I thought you were going to talk about the Emperor. I understand you knew him well."

Buxby lit up his pipe and stood to look out his window at San Francisco Bay. He puffed a smoke ring. "Don't you get it? Gerald, you said your name was? That was September 16, 1859. Exactly thirty years ago today. In two days from now it will be the thirtieth anniversary of the Emperor's first royal proclamation. No doubt that's why your editor sent you all the way up here to get this story.

"It was the next day that Joshua Norton went down to the offices of the *Evening Bulletin* and handed in his edict proclaiming himself Emperor of California. His proclamation was published the next day. . Most people think it was the loss of his fortune that drove Norton mad. That wasn't it at all. It was the duel that tipped him over the edge, the last duel ever fought in San Francisco. Come to that, I wonder if Norton was mad at all?"

Gerald cleared his throat. "He'd have to be, wouldn't he? Anyway, wasn't it because he lost his money in the rice business?"

"Oh, that." Buxby turned and resumed his seat in the leather armchair. He gave the reporter a look that made him feel he was about to laugh at him. "I suppose that had something to do with it," he said. "Everyone knows that tale. Norton was doing well for himself. He'd made a fortune speculating in real estate. He owned a rice mill. Then there was the famine in China that drove up the cost of rice. So Norton bought rice futures. He purchased the entire cargo of the *Glyde* out of Peru, before she even reached port. Then when the ship finally arrived, several other shiploads of rice sailed in at the same time. The price plummeted.

Norton went to court, trying to get out of the deal. He would have done better to take the loss, what with legal fees and court costs. In the end, he was bankrupt. But he was not a madman yet. He tried several other jobs, selling real estate and so on. No, it was the duel that pushed him over the edge. That, and the woman." "What woman?" Gerald frowned. "He never married—"

"No, but that doesn't mean he was immune to the fair sex. Actually, there were two women." Buxby leaned over and pulled a photo album from the shelf. He flipped it open and held it so the reporter could see. "Do you know who that is?"

"No Sir, I don't."

"Well, you're not from around here, are you? You're from the South, I take it. She was quite notorious for a time. Her name before she married was Sophia Andrea Hull. She's in the mad house these days, or so I'm told." Buxby flipped to another page. This one held the tintype of another woman. "This is the singer, Marina. Surely you have heard of her?"

Gerald nodded. "Of course I've heard of her, Sir. Who

hasn't? But how does she figure in the story?"

Buxby turned the book around, as if to gaze into the woman's eyes. "She was a protégée of Lotta Crabtree, who in turn was tutored by Lola Montez. Quite a line of descent. Norton had already decided to become insane by the time he met Marina, but both she and Sophia helped him along."

The reporter began to feel he was getting in over his head. He had come up here to get a few personal anecdotes about the Emperor. Instead, he sensed he was about to become entangled in a web of intrigue. Judge Buxby had poured him a snifter of brandy, which he had not touched. On an impulse, he picked it up now and took a long swig.

"You see," Buxby said, "it was like this…"

* * *

Joshua left the music hall around three in the afternoon. That new singer, Marina, was amazing. As good as Crabtree, maybe better. Joshua could not afford to buy a ticket, but he got in for free by working part time as an usher.

"How the mighty have fallen," he said out loud, referring to himself. He wondered what he ought to do about his next meal. He'd been turned down in his bid for the job of city tax collector. Not that he was surprised about that. These days, you had to know someone to get a job with the city. Strolling down Dupont Street, he came upon a large crowd of people on the sidewalk. They were nearly silent, waiting outside the office of the *Evening Bulletin*. There was something strange about this party, standing motionless, with only the sounds of low mutters and whispering. Joshua approached the nearest man, a well-off businessman or banker, judging by his coat and top hat. Joshua inquired what was going on.

"An outrage," the man said. "Senator Bradley has been shot by Justice Perry. It's said he will not live."

"Shot?" Joshua had trouble taking in the word. "But why?"

The man scowled. "A duel, they call it. It wasn't a duel, it was an assassination. Surely you know Perry is one of those Chivalrists. The pro-slavery party. They're no friend of working men like yourself. Bradley's an abolitionist, that's why Perry was out to get him. And to think they were once pals."

Joshua wondered for a moment why this stranger had taken him for a working man. Then he glanced down at his own threadbare clothes and understood the reason.

"Will he get away with it, you think? Perry, I mean."

The stranger shrugged. "These days anyone can get away with anything. Or think they can. Perry must think himself a king." He turned away.

Joshua continued his long walk back to his rooming house. He was troubled. The world was not right. He had been an honest man all his life; he should not be bankrupt and poor. These violent quarrels should not occur in a civilized nation. Wicked men believed themselves kings. There should be a solution. There should be someone capable of setting things aright. A genuine, benevolent king.

A moment arrived, as he reached Commercial Street, when the answer came to him.

* * *

It was two days later that the youthful attorney entered the offices of the *Bulletin* and asked to speak to the editor. It was his first experience of the inside of a newspaper office. He hoped it would be his last. The place was cacophony and chaos, with reporters and copyists shouting across the room at each other, the smell of ink, and scraps of paper scattered all over the place. Someone came through the door from the back room, allowing entrance for the clatter and roar of the steam powered press. The lawyer thought he might go mad, working in a place like this.

He was kept waiting ten minutes before the editor escorted him to his office. Though he closed the door, the din

was barely muffled. The editor was round, with a shiny scalp.
He was smoking a cigar. He shook the lawyer's hand.

"Bannock's my name. And you would be…?"

"Buxby," the lawyer said, "from the firm of Slater and
Woodrow. I won't take up much of your time, Mr. Bannock. It
was good of you to spare me a minute; I can see you're busy."
He held up a copy of yesterday's *Bulletin*. "I came to inquire
as to the meaning of this."

Bannock glanced at the front page. There was a notice
framed in black. The heading was, "Do We Have an Emperor
Among Us?"

> *At the peremptory request of a large majority of the
> citizens of these United States, I, Joshua Norton, formerly
> of Algoa Bay, Cape of Good Hope, and now for the past
> nine years and ten months of San Francisco, California,
> declare and proclaim myself Emperor of these U.S., and in
> virtue of the authority thereby in me vested, do hereby
> order and direct the representatives of the different States
> of the Union to assemble in the Musical Hall of this city on
> the 1st day of February next, then and there to make such
> alterations in the existing laws of the Union as may
> ameliorate the evils under which the country is laboring,
> and thereby cause confidence to exist, both at home and
> abroad, in our stability and integrity.*
> *September 1859*

Bannock handed back the paper. "Sort of a joke," he
explained. "Something to lighten the mood. The city is about
to come to a boil over that duel. Most folks are outraged
against the Chivalrists, and 'specially against Perry. Some are
calling for a new Vigilante Committee. We thought this little
item might give folks a chuckle, sort of cool off the steam, as
it were."

"But   how,   exactly,   did   you   come   by   this proclamation?" Buxby asked. "Did it really come from Joshua Norton?"

Bannock shrugged. "That's who he said he was. Came in late in the evening, as I was about to go home. He handed me this paper. Very neatly lettered, it was. He said he was the new Emperor, and could we please publish the notice. I wasn't sure if he was serious or not. He didn't look like any madman I ever met, and I've met a few. Anyway, we needed a filler for the next day's front page, so in it went. As you can see, all the rest is about the duel."

"I see. Thank you, Mr. Bannock. You have been most helpful. You see, our firm represents some of Mr. Norton's creditors. We suspect he may have considerable funds squirreled away somewhere. This so-called proclamation could be a gesture on his part, preliminary to a plea of insanity, to get out of paying his rightful debts."

Bannock took the cigar from his mouth, scratched his chin under the beard. He looked thoughtful. "You could be right. That there, might make an interesting story for the paper. But maybe you ought to talk to Norton himself. Do you know where to find him?"

Buxby sighed. "Yes, I'm afraid I do."

* * *

Joshua turned slowly, regarding himself in his mirror, examining the effect with a critical eye. Yes, he decided the peacock feather was a nice royal touch. Not too ostentatious, but enough of a flare to seize attention. He had done well to cultivate a friendship with soldiers over at the Presidio; now it was paying off. They had donated the uniform to his wardrobe. A beaver hat with cockade completed the royal outfit. Now he would not go out among his subjects unrecognized. Of course he would have preferred to carry a saber, but since that was illegal he supposed an umbrella would have to do. Finally satisfied with his appearance, he turned to the door of his room just as a knock sounded from the other side. He opened to confront a young, beardless man in a black suit.

"I'm sorry," Joshua said, "I won't be holding court today. I was on my way out to conduct an inspection of the sidewalks."

The man nodded, looking past Joshua's shoulder at the seedy room.

"Ah. I see. Well, Mr. Norton, I wasn't planning to attend court. My name is Buxby. I'm an attorney. If you're on your way out, perhaps we might go along and have a chat? Is this where you hold court, then?"

Joshua stepped out and shut the door behind him. "Please address me properly, Mr. Buxby. You may call me Emperor. Yes, I'm afraid this is my temporary palace. I realize it's a bit modest, but it's only until I can negotiate improved quarters with one of the downtown hotels. What is it you wished to chat about?"

The two made their way out to Commercial Street, where Joshua turned in the direction of North Beach.

"Ah. Well." Buxby had begun to wonder if this fellow might not turn out to be dangerous. "The fact is, Sir, I represent some of your creditors."

"I see. Well, of course you must realize I am temporarily embarrassed. But you may inform your clients I have every intention of paying whatever debts may remain. Of course, it may be necessary to impose a special tax, but I'm sure my loyal subjects will have no objection. Look there!" Joshua suddenly stopped and bent over, to point at some crumbling bricks at the curb stone. "This sort of thing cannot be tolerated! I shall issue a proclamation!"

Buxby nodded. "You're right, certainly. But then, we have other problems besides sidewalks—"

"You are correct. As Emperor, I shall not shun my responsibilities, large or small. For example, we have this sort of thing." He stopped to point his umbrella across the street, where a small gathering clustered around a man standing on a soapbox, in the middle of a sandlot. He was loudly orating to the small crowd, but only a few words were coherent, including "Bradley," "Perry," and "hanging."

"Pah," Joshua spat on the ground. "Sandlot politics. That's how Brannan got started, the bastard."

"You don't care for Sam Brannan?" Buxby asked. Brannan was one of the leading citizens of the city—one of its founders.

"You don't know him as I do. I was in the Committee of Vigilance, you see. It was Brannan that started and led the thing. I joined up because I wanted to see law and order, and we had not been getting much of that. But I quit when they started hanging fellows. They never should have done that without a trial."

"True enough, but then the city has put that sort of thing behind us—"

"You know how Brannan got his start?" Joshua seemed not to have heard. "He came out here as advance guard for the Mormons. But then he decided to steal the Mormon money and set up business for himself. Most folks have forgotten about that."

"Yes, but—"

"It was Brannan as started the Gold Rush, you know." Joshua's voice changed to a softer tone, as if he had begun to reminisce. "His idea, so he could sell more stuff from his hardware store. He walked up and down the street waving a gold nugget and yelling. A year later there were thousands of immigrants. Including myself."

Buxby glanced at the other, growing more curious. "I didn't know. You arrived here in 1849, then. Ten years ago. Right at the start."

"I believe I mentioned that in my proclamation. See here, Sir. Are you hungry by any chance? Right up ahead is one of the finest lunch counters in this neighborhood. I recommend the soup."

Buxby allowed as he was becoming peckish. The two men stopped and ate their soup slowly, standing up on the sidewalk. The food was passed over the counter to them from within. They both took time to view the passersby, afoot and by wagon. Joshua seemed intent on eating, and Buxby had trouble thinking of more conversation.

"Drat," Joshua said. "Those damned dogs." Two obviously flea ridden curs had just strolled over from around the corner. "Lazarus and Bummer," he said. "For some reason, people seem to think they belong to me. Or maybe the dogs think so. I can't stand the mongrels." He tore off two pieces of bread and tossed one to each; the food disappeared in an instant.

"Noblesse oblige," Joshua told Buxby. "One takes care of one's subjects, even those one despises. By the way, the lunch here is fifteen cents. I'm sorry to trouble you, but—"

"Yes, I know. You're momentarily embarrassed." Buxby tossed a coin to the counter man. "Shall we walk on?"

* * *

In the next several days, Joshua began to realize both the burdens and privileges of being Emperor. As he strolled down Market Street or in the commercial district, he noticed that people regarded him with respectful glances; men sometimes tipped their hats, while ladies often smiled. He always bowed in return. Items about him began to appear in newspapers. He tried to keep up with the news as much as possible though it was not easy, what with twelve daily papers to choose from. He found much of the news disturbing, especially on the national level. With the new stage run from St. Louis, it took only three weeks to get news from the East, where before it had taken two months. He wasn't sure this was a good thing.

Now and then, restaurant owners would allow him a free meal, if business was slack. One day he passed one of the better downtown establishments and noticed a sign in the window:

By appointment to his Majesty, Emperor Norton

He smiled and reminded himself to return here on a weekly basis, at least till they tired of him. On this particular evening, he was on his way to the music hall to see if he might cadge his way in; Marina was performing once again. He could not get enough of her voice.

There was a short line-up outside the box office. Being magnanimous, he did not insist on going to the front, but took his place at the end. The crowd for this matinée appeared to be thin; he hoped Marina was not losing her audience. In a few minutes he reached the ticket window and handed over a bill.

"One seat for the balcony, if you please."

The ticket seller was a fellow of about forty wearing a shirt with sleeve garters and no jacket. He had not shaved recently. He held the banknote up to the light, squinting at it.

"What do you call this?"

"That, my fellow," Joshua replied, "is legal tender in the amount of fifty cents, issued personally by Joshua Norton, Emperor of the United States and Protector of Mexico, that person being myself." He gave a short bow. He heard someone approach behind him, but did not turn around. The fellow in the box looked at the bill again, then shoved it back.

"Nice printing job, but I'm afraid we can't accept this, Your Highness."

"Now see here, Sir—perhaps you would be good enough to provide your name?" He gave the fellow an authoritative glare.

"No, I would not," the other began. But the woman standing behind Joshua interrupted.

"What's all this?"

The ticket man, with a sour face, looked past Joshua's shoulder.

"A loony trying to get in for nothing, Miss Marina."

Joshua spun about, nearly losing his balance. Then, collecting himself, he bowed. "My Lady, I had never dreamed to meet you in person. I have been your admirer and devotee for some time. I am—"

"Yes, I know who you are, Sir. I have heard about you. You would be the Emperor. There was a drawing of you in the *Morning Call.* May I see that note you were using to buy a ticket?" The ticket man passed it across; Marina studied it with care. "Ah, yes. Fifty cents. That looks legitimate to me. Please give the gentleman a ticket, Hugo. And since the matinée is only thirty-five cents, you owe him some change. I shall keep this bill as a souvenir of our meeting. Perhaps we shall meet again, Sir." She held out her gloved hand, which Joshua bowed over and kissed.

Though the theater was half empty, her voice that day was superb.

Chapter 2

The city seethed with turmoil just beneath its surface. There were fist fights, brawls, and near-riots between abolitionists and pro-slavery factions, the Chivalrists. Justice Perry, formerly of the State Supreme Court, having requested a change of venue, got his trial in Marin County for the murder of Bradley. He was acquitted, and the papers reported he'd left town for the South. Joshua read the papers, pondered, and discussed events with strangers he met on the streets. He also heard a lot of anti-Chinese talk in the streets. He wondered what he might do to bring about peace.

The year of 1859 drew somehow to a close. Before it ended, Joshua heard of another horror: John Brown hanged in Virginia. He discussed the matter at some length with Bannock at the *Bulletin,* before deciding to take action.

"This is wrong," Joshua said. "Very wrong."

"How so?" Bannock asked. "Not that I disagree, but I'd like to hear your thinking…Emperor."

"It's wrong to hang a man who's obviously insane. He should have been sent to a madhouse."

"I suppose so. But what makes you conclude he was mad? There's many another what thinks he was in his sound mind."

"He knew he was right. Only an insane man knows he is right. Those not crazy have doubts. Brown knew he was right until the very end. The fact that he *was* right has little to do with the matter. We should have compassion for those who never doubt themselves."

"Do you ever doubt yourself?" Bannock asked.

"No Sir, I do not." Joshua turned to go, then stopped. "I shall issue a proclamation tomorrow," he said. "I am dismissing Governor Wise from his post in the Province of Virginia. I shall name his successor in due course."

"There's someone you ought to meet," Bannock said.

"And who might that be, Sir?"

"A lady. Her name is Mary Ellen. She's head of the underground railroad in California."

"I shall look forward to meeting her," Joshua said.

* * *

February came and went. None of the legislators he had summoned showed up at the music hall on the indicated date. Something would have to be done. Marina was off somewhere, touring the country. He would have liked to hear her opinions. One of the people he did get to converse with was that lawyer Buxby, who had taken to dropping by Joshua's rooming house once or twice a month.

"I see you have had your portrait done," Buxby said, indicating the Daguerreotype on the mantelpiece.

"Ah, yes," Joshua smiled. "Rather flatters me, don't you think? I felt it proper that a person of my rank should have a state portrait. It cost me all of twenty-five cents."

Buxby nodded in appreciation. "Did you know that my firm had hired a Pinkerton man to follow you?"

"No. A Pink? What on earth for? Do they think me some sort of criminal?" Joshua was astounded.

"No Sir, it's not that. It's more about what we have discussed before. You are aware that certain parties, among your creditors that is, are persuaded that you may have hidden assets." Buxby sat down and picked up the cup of tea that the Emperor had graciously provided. "If I may be frank, there are some who believe your display of indigence may be a ruse to conceal hidden wealth. That you are, in crude terms, a miser. Please do not take offense, Sir. I only repeat what certain persons might say."

Joshua gave a loud snort. "Indigence, you say? That's absurd. Am I not paying fifty cents a day rent here? Are not my needs being met? Of course, it is true your rightful sovereign should have more dignified surroundings, but I am hardly indigent. By the way, perhaps you would like to invest in another of my private bonds? Seven percent interest guaranteed. I happen to have some fresh one dollar bonds…"

Buxby sipped his tea. "Perhaps after payday. At any rate, I was going to say that your Pinkerton tail has been discontinued. It was determined that you are not spending profligate amounts of cash, nor could any clue to your concealed treasure be found. Still, I am in a quandary myself. I don't know what to make of you, Sir."

Joshua turned and stared out the window. "Sometimes I don't either," he said.

* * *

Having considered with care the problems afflicting the nation as well as the state, Emperor Norton resolved to issue a proclamation demanding the army arrest the Congress. He had already abolished that legislative body, but the damned curs continued to meet, ignoring his orders. Perhaps arresting these villains would stop some of the fist fights and wrangling in Washington. Having drawn up a first draft on foolscap and made corrections, he carried it down to his friends at the *Evening Bulletin*. Bannock read it over twice, looking serious.

"This is indeed a grave matter, Emperor. It will appear in tomorrow's edition. I shall also post it on the board out in front. Are you sure this is the right thing to do?"

Joshua shrugged. "I see no other course, in these circumstances. I realize an even greater burden will fall upon my own shoulders but these problems of preserving the Union, and the issue of slavery, must be resolved somehow. It's obvious Congress can't or won't deal with them."

Bannock nodded. "There's talk in the South of secession. Of leaving the Union."

"So I've heard. That would be a tragedy, but there may be no way to prevent it. Surely no one would be fool enough to go to war over it."

"I should hope not. By the way, there was a lady here

inquiring after you."

"A lady, you say? Who might that be? And why would she come here to inquire?"

Bannock grew a thin smile. "Sophia Andrea Hull, her name is. She came here because she doesn't know where you live. I told her we are not free to divulge that information. But she left her card in case you should appear." He turned, went back to his office, and came back a minute later. He handed Joshua a nicely engraved pasteboard. "She says you should feel free to call upon her."

"Thank you, Sir. Any idea why?"

"No. But she's quite beautiful, I must say."

Joshua stared a moment at the calling card. It was unusual for a strange lady to leave a card for a gentleman. Usually it was the other way around. He pocketed the card and turned to go.

"By the way," Bannock said. Joshua halted and turned. "Sir?"

"Perhaps I ought to let you know. I believe it is common knowledge—she is the mistress of Senator David Shields."

"Ah. Well, I'm sorry to have to put the man out of his job." He tucked his umbrella under his arm and strode out the door.

* * *

Sophia at first was puzzled when her maid announced a man at the door of her apartment, waiting to see her. It had been more than a week since her visit to the *Bulletin;* she had completely forgotten her invitation. She had been terribly busy with arrangements for Senator Shields next trip to the city this coming weekend. This occasion was to include a formal soirée in the hotel dining room.

Her maid handed her a calling card engraved: *H.R.H. Joshua Norton, Emperor of U.S. and Protector of Mexico.* Then she remembered.

"Please show the gentleman to the parlor," she said. "I will only be a moment." The maid turned to go, but Sophia called her back. "Tell me. How does he seem? I mean to say— does he seem at all crazy?"

The maid shrugged. "He's oddly dressed ma'm. But well-spoken, for that."

Sophia nodded and made a *shoo* gesture; the maid turned and left. Sophia inspected her image in the mirror. She supposed she looked well enough to charm an Emperor. She was aware of how to use her beauty. Still, she had doubts about this Norton person. It wouldn't do to take chances. She found her handbag on the dressing table, popped it open and inspected the small pistol within. It was one of Mr. Remington's latest designs, and she had more faith in it than in most of the men she knew. She tucked the bag under her arm and went out to greet the Emperor.

Joshua cut quite a figure, standing at attention in the parlor, beaver hat and cane under his left arm. He made a sweeping bow.

"I am here to answer your summons, my lady."

"And I am honored, in turn," she said. She invited the Emperor to sit, and ordered her maid to bring some tea.

"I am told you arrived here during the Gold Rush," she said, when they had both become comfortable.

"Indeed," Joshua responded. "Of course, that's all in the past, Madame. The rush is over. The city is becoming a different sort of place. But there are still fortunes to be made. The city has a great future. I only hope I may help it along."

"Yes. I understand you yourself amassed a considerable fortune at one time."

"True enough. It was simply a matter of wise investing. Personally, I never had to go up to the hills to dig for ore, though I wager that might be quite an adventure. But these days I am not much concerned with finances or commerce. I wish to be an enlightened ruler."

"Certainly, the country is in need of one. But please permit me to inquire—if I'm not being too personal—as to how you manage to finance your government? Through taxation? Or do you rely on your own personal savings?" Here, Sophia was fishing for the information that she was really after. She had a feeling, backed up by common rumor, that the Emperor might have concealed assets which it might be worth one's while to know about. And perhaps to acquire. She gave Norton a sweet smile, waiting for an answer.

Joshua patted his own coat pockets, searching for something. Having found it, he produced a thin sheaf of engraved documents.

"As a matter of fact, Madame, I'm happy you asked this question. In reality, there is considerable expense in managing my government, although the expense is much less than it would be to support a Congress and President. However, I have not found it necessary to impose new taxes. Instead, I can offer you a profitable investment. I happen to have with me, some of my personal bonds which pay a guaranteed income of seven percent upon maturity..." Joshua went on at some length, explaining the purpose of his bonds. Somehow Sophia found herself holding several in her hands. She found them artistically designed. Finally, she waved a hand to stop his spiel.

"I'll take ten dollars worth," she said. Joshua looked pleased, though serious. Sophia passed him a ten dollar coin, which he quickly pocketed.

After that, she got rid of him as quickly as possible, though politely. When he had departed she went to her dressing table and got out her journal. She dipped a pen in ink, thought for a few moments, then wrote:

Emperor Norton is an enigma. He seems quite rational and not at all mad, except about his own station in life. He will bear watching. I shall endeavor to obtain his confidence. It's quite possible he may have a fortune hidden somewhere. I wonder if his bonds actually will be worth anything.... I must get busy for the soirée this weekend. I'm sure I can soon talk David into marriage.

* * *

Joshua, leaving the hotel, felt prosperous with ten dollars in his pocket. He reflected that wealth is a matter of viewpoint. A pauper may feel rich with a few dollars, while a millionaire may feel he is ruined if half his fortune disappears. He decided to indulge himself with lunch in Chinatown. Most white people he knew wouldn't go there because they considered it dirty and dangerous, but its residents were, after all, his subjects. They usually made him feel welcome, though his laundryman refused him credit.

At any rate, it was time for another inspection. He crossed Market Street, observing the pavement and watching the horse cars. He continued his stroll for several blocks North, till he reached the edge of the Chinese district. He nodded and tipped his hat to a small group of older gentlemen dressed in black. Some of them smiled back. Others merely looked at him without expression. He walked further on, growing hungry. He had hoped Miss Hull might offer lunch, but he held no resentment, since she'd been good enough to purchase his bonds. He wondered which place he should choose for his meal. There were plenty of lunch counters and restaurants to select from, as well as pushcart vendors. Finally, he settled on a place that looked clean and busy, always a good sign. He went in and took his seat at a table. There were a lot of Orientals in the place, as well as a couple of sailors nearby, speaking Russian. A waiter approached and handed him a card printed with characters.

Joshua smiled. "I'm afraid I can't read, my friend. You speak English, do you?"

The waiter shrugged. "Sure. What you want?"

"What would you recommend?"

The waiter, unsmiling, said something in Cantonese.

"Fine, I'll have that," Joshua said.

While waiting for his meal, Joshua observed everything around him. After all, this was part of his job as Emperor—being aware of what went on in his kingdom. As he was watching the crowd in the street, a white man walked by. The man glanced in the restaurant, started to walk on, then looked back and stopped. He came in and went to Joshua's table. It was Bannock, the newspaperman.

"Emperor," he said. "You turn up in the strangest places. Mind if I sit down?"

"Not at all, Sir. Would you care for some lunch? Or perhaps tea? My treat today."

"Perhaps a little tea. I wouldn't dare eat the food in this place." He paused as the waiter served Joshua with a large bowl of noodles, vegetables, and some kind of fish. Joshua had, through necessity, learned the art of eating with chopsticks. Chinatown was the most economical place to purchase a meal, but they were short on forks or spoons. He began devouring his lunch.

"And what," he said between mouthfuls, "if I may ask, brings you to this neighborhood, Mr. Bannock?"

Bannock poured himself a cup of tea. "News, of course. I can't trust any of my reporters to dig up the real stuff. They're all greenhorns. They work for me till they can find better jobs. There's rumors about a tong war. I came down here to do some snooping. Also to see my doctor."

"Your doctor, Sir? You are ill?"

" Nothing too serious, just a touch of lumbago. I won't go near those uptown medicos. Most of them can't tell one body cavity from another. But there's a Chinese doc down here who's done me some good. Dr. Luk, by name."

"A lucky sounding name. Perhaps I might consult this gentleman myself. Does he charge much?"

That was how Joshua Norton came to know Dr. Luk.

* * *

"Weak lung chi," the doctor said. Joshua lay on a table with his coat off. They were on the second floor of the building. Dr. Luk had been examining Joshua for more than half an hour. He had taken his pulse on both wrists, examined his ears, thumped his chest and peered at his tongue. He was not like any other doctor Joshua had met. Joshua sat up and adjusted his suspenders.

"I don't have any breathing problems, Doctor. It's just I have some trouble sleeping. Perhaps some laudanum...?"

Dr. Luk brushed off the sleeve of his own jacket. He spoke with a cultured English accent, as if he'd spent some time in London.

"No laudanum. I shall prepare a medicine for you. You have very weak lung chi, with excess yin. The lungs are the seat of the emotion of sadness. This is why you are unable to sleep. You have too much sadness."

Joshua was startled. He never thought of his own sadness, much less talked about it. But he could not deny it.

"There are reasons to be unhappy these days—"

Dr. Luk had turned around and was mixing herbs from several different jars. He said, "You are sad first, and find reasons. It is not the reasons that make you sad. You take this medicine home, boil it in a crockery pot for ten minutes, no more. Then you drink."

"Thank you, Doctor. How much do I owe you?"

"One dollar. You come back in a week. Maybe we do some acupuncture."

"What's that? Oh, never mind, I suppose I'll find out." He put on his coat. "Dr. Luk, as you may be aware, I am Emperor of the United States. Did you know that?"

The doctor merely shrugged, without expression. He seemed to be waiting for Joshua to leave.

"As such, I am responsible for the wellbeing of my subjects, including the residents of Chinatown. I was wondering if you might tell me something of conditions here. How goes it for the people? Are they prosperous and peace loving?"

Dr. Luk stared at him for a moment. "We are well enough," he said, "if left alone to do our work. But we are not always left alone."

"Ah. Well, Doctor, I thank you again. I can see you have patients waiting. Perhaps we may converse again?"

"Perhaps."

* * *

He saw the doctor again a week later. He tried to pay with one of his own Imperial dollar bills, but this Dr. Luk refused. Joshua gave him some of his hard-won silver instead. This time the doctor did not seem quite as rushed. He had inserted some tiny needles into Joshua's back, and answered a few questions while his patient lay there. In fact they had a rather lengthy discussion, comparatively speaking. Joshua began to understand matters he had not thought of before.

"In what way did you become Emperor?" Dr. Luk asked him without warning.

Joshua turned his head, to watch him mixing herbs. "Do you mean when? No. I suppose that's not what you meant. Perhaps you mean by what authority?" He closed his eyes. He was feeling relaxed and peaceful, in fact better than he'd felt in weeks. He had never considered this question, nor had anyone asked it of him. The doctor continued mixing herbs, perhaps awaiting an answer, perhaps not.

"It was that duel," Joshua answered at last. "You remember? When Perry killed Bradley? I asked myself how a man could get away with such a crime. And him a prominent citizen, no street thug. Back in the days of the Vigilantes, we used to hang murderers, gangsters like the Sydney Ducks. Perry was against the Vigilance Committee. He stood for law and order, but he stabbed a man with his Bowie knife. He got away with it.

You see, Doctor, if a man says he's a judge and claims authority, he may do anything he wishes. If he says he is right, then he is right, because people believe it so. I claim the right to be Emperor, and to use my powers for good, not evil. I am Emperor because I believe it, as do the people, my subjects." He fell silent. Dr. Luk turned to him and began removing the needles. He had no comment.

* * *

The next day, Joshua heard that Marina was back in the city. He was running short on cash, and had doubts that one of his personal banknotes would work a second time. So he strolled down to the music hall and waited by the stage door in back, hoping to catch a glimpse of her as she made her exit. On his way, he had gathered a bunch of poppies from a vacant lot, for a bouquet. This was not one of her personal concerts; she was appearing on stage in a variety show which included a string quartet and a recitation of Shakespeare. Joshua took his seat on an empty pickle barrel in the alleyway. Through an open window, he could just make out the muffled orations of Shakespeare. He smiled, remembering another Shakespearian event he had once witnessed in this very hall.

He was still sitting there an hour later when Marina came out the door. He had been privileged to hear her sing an aria from *Cosi Fan Tutti*. His heart all but broke, listening.

"Ah, Mr. Emperor," she said as she appeared outside. He leapt to his feet, startled, not having expected her so soon.

"What delightful flowers. For me? Perhaps you could do me the honor of escorting me to my hotel," she said. "I'm afraid I can't afford a cab today, but it's only a few blocks. I should enjoy the stroll."

He bowed, sweeping his hat and peacock feather. "An honor, Madame. But I thought you would have stayed for the final curtain call."

She made a dismissive gesture with her fan. "I shouldn't bother, not with what they're paying me. Perhaps I should have accepted that offer to tour in Europe, but matters are so unstable these days. I thought California might be safer. But how have you faired, Your Majesty? Did you hear me sing today?"

He smiled. "Indeed. You were heavenly. I also caught some of the Shakespeare, which reminded me of an incident several years ago. There was a company performing 'Scenes From Shakespeare.' The audience was made up largely of families, with children." He paused to point upward toward Telegraph Hill.

"As you know, that semaphore is used to communicate with ships entering and leaving the bay, as well as to let the harbor master know what ships are arriving. Of course, all the young boys in town have learned to understand the signals. Well. During this theatrical performance of which I speak, an actor rushed onto stage, spreading his arms wide, like this." Joshua stopped to demonstrate.

"Whereupon he declaimed, *What meaneth this, my Lord?* Immediately, a red-headed Irish lad shouted, *Side-wheel steamer!*"

Marina stared at him a moment, then burst into laughter, until tears came to her eyes. When she was able to speak again she said, "Emperor Norton! You have made me laugh for the first time in weeks! How can I repay you?"

He bowed. "Madame, hearing your gaiety is reward enough."

"Nevertheless, you shall dine with me this evening, and I don't care what the public may think."

* * *

Marina felt generous and in a spending mood. She took him that evening to a high-toned restaurant located in the Montgomery Block, the place most locals called The Monkey Block.

"What's money for, if not to spend?" she laughed. "You made me smile, you deserve a reward." Joshua had no objection to luxury. She ordered champagne while they studied the menus. She said, "I recommend the abalone." He ordered that, as well as poached sole. Marina asked for lamb chops. He said, "I take it you have been unhappy of late."

"Who wouldn't be?" she said. "Do you read the papers? There's a good chance Mr. Lincoln and the Republicans will be elected. Surely you know what has happened in Kansas. I was touring the South—New Orleans and Atlanta, among other places. But I decided to cut it short—there's so much anger there. They don't look kindly on Yankees these days."

Joshua drew lines on the tablecloth with his finger. He said, "Would that I could help. The Congress persists in holding their meetings, despite my orders. And the army also ignores my proclamations. I could issue a proclamation freeing the slaves, but I fear it would be ignored as well."

Marina leaned across the table, gazing directly into his eyes. She spoke in a lower tone. "Emperor, I wonder, might I ask a question without your taking offense? For surely, you know I do not mean to offend."

He lifted a silver spoon to sip delicately at his soup. "Please ask, dear lady."

She glanced about the room, as if to make sure no one overheard. The restaurant was not crowded, but it was becoming busy. She spoke in a low tone: "I know you do read the newspapers, Emperor. Surely you have seen the articles they write about you. And the cartoons. Do you know they are making fun of you? Laughing at you?"

"Do they?" He continued sipping at his soup.

She shrugged. "Well, yes. But I see that doesn't bother you. Perhaps those jackals of the press are simply too far beneath you for notice. If that be the case, you have my support."

"Thank you, my dear."

"Emperor," she continued in the same tone, "they say

you're crazy. Do you think that's true?"

He looked up at her. "Quite possibly." He smiled.

"Who's that headed this way?" Glancing past his shoulder. "Oh, yes, I know her."

Joshua turned as the other lady approached, then pushed back his chair to stand.

"Please don't rise," Sophia said. "I just came by to say hello. If I'm not mistaken, this is the famous Marina. We met two seasons ago, when you were in *Don Giovanni*. How charming to find you both together—two of San Francisco's most famous citizens. Do you come here often?"

"Rarely, I'm afraid," Marina said. "I have been on tour, only just returned. But I do hope to remain awhile."

"I hope you will accept an invitation to my next soirée. Perhaps you could both come. But you must excuse me, I see my escort is becoming impatient over there. I only dropped by to say hello. Enjoy your evening."

Marina watched her retreating back. "There's something about that woman that grates on me."

"I found her agreeable," he said. "She bought some of my bonds."

* * *

From the journal of Sophia Andrea Hull:

Now I am convinced. The matter is settled. This evening I discovered Emperor Norton dining formally at the Monkey Block in the company of a local theater woman, a diva named Marina. I'm sure she doesn't come cheap. If Norton can afford to wine and dine celebrities in such an establishment, then he is no pauper. He must have a concealed treasure somewhere. I think I shall get to know this gentleman better. Perhaps I shall speak to that trollop as well.

Chapter 3

Buxby, as a junior attorney, could not afford a rooming house equipped with a bath. Therefore, once a week or so, he chose to journey to the What Cheer House at California and Montgomery streets. This was one of the better hotels, equipped with a public bath in the basement. He enjoyed soaking in the iron tub for an hour, breathing in steam and the scent of strong soap. He especially enjoyed the experience during cold, damp weather, which could happen at any time of year in this city.

Today, after his soak, he emerged to street level to encounter the Emperor, striding down the street as if with certain purpose. Buxby tipped his hat.

"Where away, Your Majesty? In a hurry?"

Joshua stopped and bowed. "Not at all, Sir. Merely enjoying the day. Of course, I'm inspecting my sidewalks at the same time. I think we could use some new planking along here."

"Well, Sir. If you've nothing urgent in mind, perhaps you would care to accompany me. I'm on my way to a lecture, if I'm not late."

"Why not? What sort of lecture?"

"It's a lady, Mary Ellen by name. Perhaps you have heard of her?"

"The name strikes a chord. Lead on, my friend. I am eager always to learn."

The lecture hall belonged to the San Francisco chapter of the Workingman's Union. It was not large, and the crowd filled it almost to capacity. Buxby and Joshua took their seats at the rear, amid a murmur of discussion. They had not long to wait. A man in laborer's clothes stepped up to the podium and gave a brief introduction; then Mary Ellen swept in from backstage.

"A handsome lady," Joshua commented. Buxby nodded, while the crowd fell silent. Mary Ellen launched into a prepared talk about the slavery question and the rights of Negroes. A few minutes into her speech, someone from the audience passed a note to her. She paused, glanced at it, then raised her hand.

"Friends," she said. "Ladies and gentlemen. I am told we are honored today by the presence of the Emperor of the United States and Protector of Mexico, His Royal Highness Joshua Norton the First. We are truly blessed."

Joshua rose and gave a solemn bow in the lady's direction, among a smattering of giggles and laughter. Mary Ellen raised her hand again as Joshua sat down.

"Those of you who laugh," she said, "you had best think again. Is our Emperor any more ridiculous than those who pretend to govern us from Washington? Or, for that matter, anyone in this room?" She paused a moment until the hall was quiet once more, then returned to her speech. A few of those in the audience turned to give Joshua curious glances, then appeared to forget him as they became caught up in the lady's message.

Her speech was impassioned, fiery, and to the point. It was evident she had no patience with subtlety. There were still men in the halls of Congress who would make California a slave state, and she had no patience with them either. When she was finished, there was a standing ovation. When she left the stage, her audience burst into a hundred loud arguments. Buxby and Joshua rose to make their departure. A large man with a beard, a roughneck by the look of him, barred their way. He handed Joshua a slip of paper.

Dear Emperor—Buxby *read over Joshua's shoulder*—*I should be interested in hearing your viewpoint. Please come to the parlor behind the stage. The bearer of this note will conduct you. I look forward to the pleasure of your visit.* ...Mary Ellen

Buxby grinned and slapped Joshua on the shoulder. "You seem to have made an impression with the lady. You go on back. I believe I shall go to the Monkey Block for a quiet drink." He turned and disappeared into the crowd.

Joshua followed his burly guide to a side door and through a long corridor to a room at the rear. He found Mary Ellen ensconced on a sofa. She rose to give him a formal curtsy.

"Your Highness. We have often passed each other in the street, and I have long wanted to meet you. Please sit and have some lemonade. What did you think of my speech?"

He bowed and sat on the edge of an upholstered chair, tugging at his trousers so as not to have the knees bag.

"I found it quite inspiring, though I admit there were certain parts I found difficult to understand—never having been in the South. And other parts I found disturbing."

"Disturbing?" she raised an eyebrow. "Such as?"

"Pardon me if I misunderstand. You seemed to be calling for military action. For a state of war, that is."

She took a sip of her lemonade, then gave him a serious look. "My dear Emperor, we have been in a state of war since John Brown was hanged. What I am calling for is more decisive action and better leadership. Some of us pin our hopes on Lincoln, but that remains to be seen."

"Ah. I must say you are forthright, but it would be a tragedy to break the Union, especially if it means shedding blood."

"It would be a greater tragedy to allow slavery to continue," she said.

Joshua stared at the carpet for a moment. "Might I inquire—if I am not too personal—how a lady such as yourself became so involved in this cause?"

She gave a short laugh, then looked serious again. "Oh, I see. You are not familiar with my own history. Tell me— judging by my accent and appearance, where would you guess

I am from?"

Joshua looked her over. He leaned his chin on his walking cane. "Well Madame, from your speech I should guess you hail from the East, perhaps Boston or maybe Philadelphia. You are clearly well educated. Beyond that, I couldn't say."

Mary Ellen leaned forward and stared, as if to mesmerize him. "My grandfather was governor of the State of Virginia," she said. My father was his son. But my mother was a slave, and a Voodoo priestess."

Joshua nodded, considering these facts.

"I was fortunate," she said. "When my mother died, I was purchased by an abolitionist family from Nantucket. They brought me North and took me into their family and gave me an education. I'm also fortunate I can pass for white. There are thousands of others who are not so lucky."

"Ah. I see," Joshua said.

They conversed a few minutes longer, or rather Joshua listened while she explained. Then she said she had another engagement. A woman came to tell her a carriage was ready, and Mary Ellen rose to go.

"Thank you for your advice and counsel," she said. "I shall value the friendship of Your Royal Highness." Then she was gone. Joshua went home to think.

* * *

The Journal of Sophia Andrea Hull:

The Senator drags his feet. He is reluctant to marry. He brings me all manner of excuses, rather than a simple ring. I know I shall pin him down sooner or later, but I begin to suspect he may have another woman hidden away somewhere, perhaps in Nevada. Ah, well. There is more than one path to fortune. I am still intrigued by the Emperor—not, Good Heavens! that I might be inclined to wed him! But I am convinced he conceals a fortune somewhere. No doubt he is biding his time until his creditors become unwary. I think he remains in this city only because he has large amounts of cash nearby. Yesterday I went to call upon his lady friend Marina, at her wretched rooming house...

* * *

Marina was surprised when her visitor was announced, since few outside the theater knew where she lived. When she came down to the parlor, she was even more taken aback to find the beautiful Sophia waiting.

"Please forgive me for my sudden appearance," Sophia said. "I should have sent a note first, but I'm afraid I'm rather impulsive; this was quite spur of the moment. I hope I am not intruding."

"Not at all," Marina smiled. "I was just resting a bit after my matinée. I have another concert later this evening, but I admit I'm surprised by your visit. May I ask as to the occasion?"

The landlady brought in a pot of tea and left again without a word. The pot had a small crack in the handle. Sophia gave it an odd glance, but Marina proceeded to pour.

"Well, I did wish to make your acquaintance," Sophia said. "I have had the pleasure of hearing you perform on many occasions, but I must admit I had another motive. I shan't beat about the bush, as they say. It's because you seem to be on such good terms with our Emperor."

Marina was puzzled. "I suppose I am, though I've only spoken to him a few times. What is it exactly that concerns you?"

Sophia broke out her fan and fluttered it, glancing out the open window. "San Francisco weather is so unpredictable, don't you think? Balmy days in winter, cold and damp in the summer. Tell me, do you think the Emperor mad?"

Marina was startled by the question. "Mad? I suppose that depends on what you mean. At times he seems quite reasonable. Certainly he's no danger."

"No, at least not to others. I will be frank, my dear. I have had occasion to observe Joshua—the Emperor—for some time now. I fear for his safety. Walking the streets in all sorts of neighborhoods, even Chinatown. A wonder he hasn't been Shanghaied. What if someone, for example, should abduct him and force him to reveal where he conceals his fortune? Don't you think he might be better off if he were somewhat, shall I say, restrained?"

"His fortune?" Marina blinked. "Restrained? I am not sure I catch your meaning. You say he has a fortune?"

Sophia opened her handbag, fumbled in it for a few seconds. She had to push under the pistol so as not to reveal it. She took out some printed bills.

"These bond notes he sells." She passed them to Marina. "Were you aware of them?"

Marina examined them closely. "I wonder where he has them printed? Yes, I knew about them, but I have not heard of anyone actually redeeming one."

"Joshua also prints his own money. I wonder if he is prepared to back his notes with silver or gold?"

Marina passed them back. "Well, Miss Hull, I must admit I'm baffled."

Sophia rose, not having touched her tea. "I shall leave you to your rest, my dear. I'm sorry to have disturbed you. I only called out of concern for our mutual friend, the Emperor. Perhaps I should not have worried you so."

"You have given me something to think about." She followed Sophia toward the door. "Perhaps you're right to be concerned."

Sophia paused before leaving. "I do have an idea. You know I would do anything to help that poor man. Just suppose you should, shall we say, sound him out regarding where he has his fortune concealed. No doubt it's all in cash, to evade the banks and his creditors. Between the two of us, likely we could find a better means of securing his wealth and protecting his person. Don't you think? Joshua is so alone, despite being such a public figure. And, I fear, a laughing stock. What he needs are true friends—such as ourselves."

And she went out the door before Marina could think of a proper response.

* * *

The Journal of Sophia Andrea Hull:

...A typical theater woman. No doubt she is after His Royal Highness's money. At least now she knows I know. On the other hand, she may actually be so naïf she hadn't considered it. In any case, I have stirred the pot. Let's see what bubbles to the surface.

* * *

Joshua watched the pot boiling in Dr. Luk's office. It was a thick clay pot with a spout, a sort of earthenware tea kettle. The aroma filling the room was heady, almost intoxicating. There was an underlying odor of licorice.

"We never use metal ware to prepare the medicine," Dr. Luk explained. "It would change the mixture." He lifted the pot from its charcoal brazier, setting it aside. "When it cools, you drink one cupful. Two cups a day until it be gone."

"What will it do for me?"

"It make you less sad."

Joshua got into his heavy uniform coat and picked up his hat. "I do seem to be sleeping better."

"I am happy to help." He got down a glass jar for carrying the mixture. "Twenty-five cents for the prescription."

Joshua rummaged in his pockets. "Dr. Luk, you have aided me greatly. I was thinking perhaps I should bestow a knighthood upon you. How embarrassing, I seem to be about fifteen cents short today. Perhaps you would accept one of my personal notes..."

Dr. Luk waved a hand. "You pay me next time. Never

mind the knight business, this ain't England."

Joshua bowed. "You are generous to extend me credit, Doctor. I shall certainly make it up at my next visit."

* * *

On his way home, with the jar in his large coat pocket, he considered that he'd have to rely on a free soup kitchen for supper today. He'd not had much luck selling bonds to tourists lately, and the better restaurants were beginning to tire of his presence. He didn't much mind the soup kitchens; there was always someone interesting to talk to—sailors from all parts of the world, as well as out of work miners and gentlemen like himself down on their luck. Just then he spotted a familiar face on the street—Mr. Bannock, of the *Bulletin*.

"Good evening, Sir," he called, catching up with him.

"Ah, the Emperor." Bannock fell into step with him. "Inspecting our public works again?"

"In a manner of speaking, Sir. And I assume you are about gathering news, as usual?"

Bannock laughed. "I would if I could find some. There are plenty of rumors. A lot of muttering in back halls. Some people clam up when they find out I'm a newsman. Have you heard anything good, yourself?"

Joshua shook his head, wondering how he might steer the conversation toward supper. "Reading the papers confuses even myself, your Ruler. There is so much dissension. I have considered issuing a proclamation dissolving the Republic. I say, what's all this ahead?"

They had turned a corner to find a small crowd surrounding a sandlot orator.

"...taking jobs away from honest working white men..." They could hear the speaker expounding. There were forty or fifty men gathered around, mostly dressed in working men's garments. A few women hovered on the outskirts of the crowd. The speaker stood on a wooden box and ranted: *"I say we arm ourselves! Let's set fire to Chinatown, burn the rascals out!"* He continued in that vein for several minutes. There were a few shouts from the crowd, mostly of approval. Fists were raised and shaken. It was evident the mob was getting worked up. Bannock turned to say something to Joshua, only to find he was no longer there. He looked about and was horrified to see him at the front of the crowd, approaching the orator.

Bannock watched while Joshua plucked at the man's sleeve and said something to him in a low tone. The man laughed. Then he spoke to the crowd.

"Sure, why not? Folks, it seems our Emperor of the U.S. here has something to say! What do you folks think? Should we let him get up here and talk?" There were raucous shouts of "Let him talk!" and "Let's hear the Emperor!" There were also some laughs. The orator got down from his box and Joshua mounted. Bannock watched from the rear with great trepidation. He was afraid to hear what Joshua was about to say. If he spoke out in support of this rabble rouser, it could result in a riot. If he were to speak against him, he would likely get himself killed.

Joshua looked out over the mob for a moment in silence. Then he placed both hands together and bowed his head. He began reciting the Lord's Prayer.

Bannock was amazed. Some of his listeners bowed their own heads and began praying with him. When Joshua got to "Amen," he began over from the beginning. Bannock stood still and listened. By the third repetition, some of the crowd began to drift away. Joshua continued praying, his voice level and calm. Bannock lost track of how many times he said the prayer. Finally there was only himself and Joshua left in the sandlot. He walked over to Joshua and reached up to tap his shoulder.

"You can stop now, Your Royal Highness. They have all gone home."

Joshua stopped, lowered his hands, looked around. He

got down from the box. He said nothing, but only nodded in satisfaction.

"This story will make tomorrow's edition," Bannock said. "What do you say to a steak dinner?"

"The Lord provides," Joshua said.

* * *

Marina read about this exploit in the next day's paper. It was on the second page; most of the first page was taken up with news from the East. Now that the Pony Express was running, it seemed local news was taking a back seat. Marina wasn't sure this was a good thing. She read the story about Joshua in the sandlot three times, then cut it carefully from the paper, to be placed later in her scrapbook. Marina did not keep a journal or diary, because she wasn't much for writing. But she kept clippings that related to her life, mostly reviews and notices of her work in theater. She was feeling these days that Joshua was somehow related to her own life. She decided to go and see him.

* * *

Sophia also made up her mind to go and see Joshua. What decided her was a message from the detective she'd hired. He wasn't a Pinkerton man — she couldn't quite afford one of those, but he was said to be good.

Miss Hull,

This fellow you are asking about has been spending a lot of time in Chinatown. He even eats there sometimes. If you can believe it. He's been going to a chink doctor about once a week. I'd wager he has some kind of undercover dealings going on there, where most white men wouldn't even think to look. I'm told this "doctor" has dealings with one or more of the local tongs. I'll see what else I can find out, but Miss Hull if you want me to go much further you are going to have to come up with some extra hazard pay. I don't want no hatchet in the back of my head. Let me know what you want.

Of course the note wasn't signed. If what this detective fellow said was true, it would make sense. Where better to conceal a fortune than in Chinatown? Even the Police didn't go there. It was even possible Norton had converted all his cash to opium; that was always salable, easily changed back to cash. Yes, she would go talk to the Emperor again. And ask him to show her Chinatown.

* * *

Marina got to him first. She had sent him a note inviting him to visit at her rooming house on Saturday afternoon. He showed up exactly on time. After the landlady served tea, she complimented him on his action at the sandlot.

"You were most courageous," she said. He blinked at her, as if trying to understand what she was talking about.

"Oh? How so?" he asked. In her turn, she stared back at him, thinking he was either brave or a complete madman. But she didn't say that. Instead, she said,

"You made the papers again, you know. After all that news from the East. They say the telegraph is coming. Soon we'll be getting news from London and Paris almost before it happens. Just think. I was reading a magazine article the other day—it said the telegraph will soon mean the end of newspapers. Everyone will have one in the home. It will print out the news automatically on a paper ribbon. Then there won't be any point in having newspapers, will there?"

Joshua frowned in thought. "I wonder who will publish my proclamations?"

Marina sipped her tea, trying to think how to broach the real reason for seeing Joshua today.

"Emperor—Your Highness. I was wondering if you might require some assistance with your personal problems."

"Which problems would those be, Madame?" He smiled. "Did you hear that the Board of Supervisors has agreed to furnish me with a new uniform? This old one is getting threadbare, unsuitable for your Ruler, wouldn't you agree?"

"Yes. Yes, I did hear that. I think it's wonderful. I'm sure your appearance will be impressive. What I was referring to is the matter of your finances."

"Ah. Perhaps you know of a possible sponsor interested in purchasing some of my bonds?" He began digging some papers from an inner pocket.

"No, that's not what I meant. I mean to say—perhaps I overstep my bounds, but you must believe I speak to you as a friend. I only wonder if you have taken adequate steps to safeguard your financial resources?" At his blank look she added, "I mean your money."

"Oh, that. Well, you know one does the best one can. But I am always open to suggestions. I'm sure you understand that in my zeal to govern the Empire well, I sometimes tend to overlook my own interests. But I hope you are not unduly concerned."

"I realize your problem with creditors. The need to conceal your funds, and so on. I was only thinking, perhaps if your cash were safe in a bank, possibly under an assumed name...But of course, I don't have much experience in these matters. If you had a good lawyer—"

Joshua abruptly got to his feet. "Madame, I am sure you have my best interests at heart, and I am touched by your concern, but I must tell you, I have little use for the law these days. I truly hope that all the lawyers I shall ever meet are in my past. With the exception, of course, of Mr. Buxby. I thank you for the tea, but I must take my departure before I have overstayed your hospitality." He made a low bow and turned to leave. Marina leaped after him.

"Oh, Joshua! I mean, Emperor! Must you leave so soon? I hope I have not offended you!"

He took her hand and kissed it. "Not in the least, my

lady. I look forward to our next conversation." And then he was gone.

* * *

Buxby dropped by Commercial Street later that week. He asked Joshua if he were planning any new proclamations.

"Not at the moment," Joshua said. He had been polishing his boots, but put them aside in deference to his guest. The room was filled with the odor of wax and bootblack. "I am awaiting developments," he said. "The nation is unstable. As is this city. There is labor unrest. The working men take out their resentments on the Chinese. And of course there's the underground railroad, which the South resents. So many people angry with each other. It's sad the Gold Rush could not last forever, but there's an end of it. What's fun is fun, what's done is done.

"No, Mr. Buxby, I have no proclamations at this moment that will solve the ills of the nation. I am Emperor by grace of God, but I am not God. I promise to let you know when I think of something."

"You do not speak at all like a madman," Buxby observed.

"Would you prefer I did?"

Buxby pulled a flask from his pocket. "Perhaps you would take a bit of heart warmer with me? The finest French cognac. Or so I'm told."

Joshua frowned. "I'm afraid I have not much taste for strong spirits. But perhaps, just a drop." Buxby poured into a couple of tiny silver cups and passed one to Joshua. Both men sipped and were silent a few moments.

"Did you know that woman Sophia is having you followed?" Buxby asked.

Joshua raised a brow. "Following me? Whatever for?"

"I'm not sure, but it may have something to do with your creditors. She has sent a hireling to our legal offices to inquire about you. From what I hear, she is of the opinion that you may be concealing unreported assets. Of course, I don't believe a word of that. But I'm told she's interested in knowing where you go, and whom you see."

Joshua laughed. "Why didn't she simply ask? I would be happy to show her. I find her a charming lady; I'd be delighted to have her company."

"She's quite beautiful. But be careful, Your Highness. One doesn't always know what lies behind a lovely face. You *don't* have concealed assets, do you?"

"Only of the spiritual kind," Joshua said. He tossed off the cognac. Then he added, "Speaking hypothetically, of course—if I were actually to possess some sort of what you term *assets,* and were I to inform you of them—well, then, there is your position. I mean to say, you would be honor bound to tell your employers, would you not? Unless, of course, I were to swear you to secrecy."

"Naturally, if I were to swear an oath—"

Joshua looked at the ceiling. "I should not wish to place you in an untenable position, my friend. On the one hand, you would be bound in honor to inform your employers. On the other, if you swore an oath, you would be bound to betray them. I could not wish such a fate on a friend."

Buxby scowled. "No. I can see that. I can see why you would not wish to tell me about your hidden assets."

"Not that I actually have any. I was speaking hypothetically."

Buxby, feeling suddenly uncomfortable, arose and took his leave. Outside, the weather was cold and drizzling.

* * *

Sophia looked out her third floor window at the rain and mist. The weather reflected her mood. She had just read the latest note from the Senator. He had decided to remain in Carson City another week or so due to "the press of business." Sophia wondered if perhaps he might be experiencing the press of some other woman's flesh. She would have to get something on him, in the event he showed signs of reneging on his various promises.

Meanwhile, she needed to keep busy. There was this intriguing affair of the Emperor. Surely there was more to the fellow than met the eye. Sophia hated mysteries, unless she could unravel them. She was determined to solve this one. She consulted her journal, where she had written down the Emperor's home address, provided by her detective. She had dismissed the detective yesterday, since he had about fulfilled his purpose. It seemed he was too timid to make inquiries in Chinatown. Sophia was not timid. Especially with a revolver in her handbag.

She would go and see Emperor Norton first thing in the morning.

* * *

The Emperor had a sleepless night. He had an intuition of something bad about to happen. He wasn't sure if it would be to him personally, or to his empire. In a sense, it was all the same. An injury to his subjects was a blow to himself. When he did doze, he had disturbing dreams he could not remember.

He awoke early, determined to take a long walk along the waterfront to clear his head. He was surprised when the landlord knocked on his door to announce a lady to see him. He was more surprised to find Sophia waiting downstairs.

She made a low curtsy. "Good morning, your Royal Highness," she said, smiling. "Would you do me the honor of taking breakfast with me?"

At the mention of breakfast, his stomach growled. He made a low bow. "I should be delighted, Madame."

She had a taxi waiting in the street: a one-horse trap. They drove back to her hotel, which had a restaurant on the ground floor. He ordered scrambled eggs, she had oysters.

"What do you think of the proposal of the Chivalrists?" she asked.

"Which proposal? You mean, to make California a

slave state?"

"No, they have quite given up on that idea. What they want now is to divide the state, only the southern part to allow slavery. To work the fields and farms, you see."

"I believe that is a stupid idea," he said.

Her expression was noncommittal. The truth was, Sophia didn't care one way or the other, unless it affected her personal fortunes. She was trying to sound him out, to understand his thinking.

"Will you issue a Royal Proclamation on the subject?"

"I may. I shall have to think about it." He was making short work of the eggs.

"I understand you have certain contacts in Chinatown," she said.

"Oh? And where did you hear that?"

She waved a hand. "Here and there. You're quite the celebrity, you know. Your public is watching. Your every move is reported in the papers, if not by word-of-mouth. Probably your breaking fast with me this morning is likely to cause gossip."

He gave a sly smile. "I should consider such gossip an honor."

"Tell me—do you mind terribly if I call you Joshua?"

He glanced around the room. "That would be quite all right, as long as we're alone. But not in public, of course."

"Oh, of course. What I wanted to ask, Joshua, if I'm not being too forward—have you ever considered marriage?"

"Marriage?" He gave her a serious look. "As a matter of fact, I have thought it might be proper for the Emperor to have a consort. But the field of eligible candidates is somewhat limited. I am considering a proposal to Queen Victoria of England. What do you think?"

She was serious in her turn. "Well. That would certainly be an advantageous match for you. But you must be aware she is already married, to that Albert fellow. And I must say, she's plain as a mud hen. If you'll forgive me."

He studied his empty plate. "Yes, there is that. Do you suppose I might have a second helping?"

* * *

He left her about ten in the morning. She made him promise to show her about Chinatown; of course a lady must not go there unaccompanied. He readily agreed, and made an appointment for Friday. The rest of their conversation was mostly small talk. Leaving Sophia, he thought she had a puzzled expression, but he couldn't make out why.

Outside, the weather was still gloomy and damp, but he didn't mind much. His woolen uniform with the golden epaulets kept him warm, though it did tend to get rumpled. He enjoyed walking in the street. Passing the music hall, he felt a tap on his shoulder. He turned to discover Marina. He bowed.

"Such a delight to encounter a charming lady on a beautiful day," he said.

She laughed. "You have never seen an ugly day, have you? Come walk with me. I was just finishing a rehearsal. A small part in a play, you know. Nothing much, but it will almost pay my rent."

He took her arm, and they began to stroll. "I shall be sure to catch your performance," he said. "By the bye, what month is this? Are we in Spring, Fall, or what?"

Marina held a gloved hand out to catch the faint drizzle. "April showers. This is April. I should have taken my umbrella. Did you really not know what month this is?"

He shrugged. "Sometimes I forget. I lose track. Being Emperor takes up so much of my mind, details like the month or year seem less important. I suppose that's a privilege of rank, now I think about it—not having to keep count of days. There are times when I feel I may never grow older, that I shall remain the same forever. But I know that isn't true. The world changes, I must change with it. Or so they say. By the bye, someone was speaking to me recently of marriage. What is your opinion of that institution?"

"Marriage? Perhaps you should ask someone else their thoughts. I was married once, you see. In fact, I still am, far as I know. That experiment was not a success."

"Ah. I'm so sorry."

"Don't be. I was quite young, he was a cad. A polished and charming man, but a cad. He was a gambler and a drinker. He ran off with a polished and charming widow with money. I heard they went to Buenos Aires."

She was silent a moment, thinking. "Speaking of change, someone at the theater mentioned there's important news from the eastern states today. Have you heard anything?"

"News?" He glanced at her. "Good or bad?"

"Isn't most news bad? That's what makes it news."

"So it is. No, I've heard nothing yet today. Suppose we take a slight detour past the office of the *Morning Call,* to see what's up?"

So they did. The *Call* was around the corner and two blocks up. Long before they reached it, they could see a crowd gathered. As usual in this city, it was a mixed group: laborers, miners, a few Chinese, some men in stovepipe hats, ladies with umbrellas. They stood about silently, straining to read the posters at the front of the building. Some newsboys were among the crowd, selling papers as quickly as they could hand them out. Oddly, they were not shouting or hawking headlines; that wasn't necessary today.

Emperor Norton pushed his way through the crowd. Most people moved aside in automatic deference to his regal bearing. He reached the front of the building and quickly scanned the nearest poster.

Marina was directly behind him, straining to see. "What does it say?"

Norton turned, looking grim. "It says, *Fort Sumter Has Been Fired Upon.*"

"Where's that?" she asked.

Chapter 4

For the next few days, the city did not boil, but it simmered.. Economic conditions had been unsettled for several years; now Panic approached. Then investors speculated wildly, buying up crop futures, anticipating Government spending on the military. The Pony Express terminal became jammed with visitors awaiting the latest news from St. Joseph, Missouri.

Bemused, Joshua scanned the newspapers, remembering his own past ventures in capitalism. Some men would grow rich from all this, while others would be ruined. The reports were confused and vague; movements of troops, militias called up. Joshua wondered what he might do to ease the situation. The Congress should have complied with his proclamation and disbanded then this mess never would have happened.

Buxby dropped in for his weekly visit. He had a newspaper under his arm. "There's an item from St. Louis about one of our former citizens," he remarked.

"Who might that be?"

"This fellow Sherman. He's been running a local railroad company back there. Says he's decided to accept a commission as colonel in the army; he'll be traveling to Washington next month, it says here. Perhaps you knew him. William Tecumseh Sherman."

"Of course." Joshua nodded. Lately, the daily news tended to make him weary. He thought perhaps he should see Dr. Luk again, for more of his concoction to make him less sad. He said to Buxby, "I recall him well. He ran a bank in town for two or three years. It failed. From what I heard, the man has failed at every endeavor. No doubt he will botch his army job as well."

"I shouldn't be surprised. What did you have planned

for today, Your Majesty?"

Joshua rose from his chair. He felt a need for some kind of action, anything. "Today is steamer day. I thought I might stroll down to the wharf to greet any new immigrants."

"Excellent idea. I shall accompany you."

The two went out together. San Francisco was not a large city; one could walk easily from one side of town to the other in two or three hours. It did not take them long to reach Meigg's Wharf. There was an unusually large crowd gathered, many of them well-dressed businessmen. A number of young men, apparently intending to debark, guarded their steamer trunks or bags. They were a curious group, some well-heeled judging by the quality of their luggage, others in workmen's clothes and shouldering canvas sacks.

Emperor Norton as usual strode through the crowd, which parted for him, Buxby at his heels. Shielding his eyes with his cap, he gazed out across the bay. A side-wheel steamer approached from just off Alcatraz.

"I see we're in time." Then, to a nearby man wearing a stovepipe hat, "Pray, Sir, what ship is that?"

"Brother Jonathan," the man replied. He glanced at Norton with no sign of surprise. "She'll be turning around for the Panama run as soon as she re-coals. Some of the men here are headed East, to join the army." He stopped and glanced around, then lowered his voice. "Some are for the South, and some for the North. Should be an interesting voyage."

"I dare say. Why are all these others here? Are we expecting special cargo?"

The man shrugged. "No more than usual in-bound, far as I know. But she'll be picking up a load of gold bars bound for Washington. Or there may be some going to the South, I wouldn't know. The prices have gone up again, gold is in demand. As for myself, I'm down from Sacramento for a shipment of farming supplieswhile it's still available. I run a dry goods store up there. No telling what will happen to commerce in the next few weeks." He turned and took a closer look at Norton, scanning him up and down. "I see you are in uniform, Sir. Would you be here on army business, then?"

Buxby stepped forward. "You are from out of town, my friend, so of course you wouldn't know. This is Joshua Norton the First, Emperor of the United States and Protector of Mexico."

"Ah. I see. Glad to make your acquaintance, Emperor." Then the stranger turned and moved quickly away, with a nervous glance over his shoulder. Buxby and the Emperor waited to see the ship dock and to watch passengers disembark.

"Not like the old days," Joshua remarked, watching a couple with three children make their way down the gangplank.

"What do you mean?"

"When I arrived here during the Rush, there were hardly any women or children. Hardly any city, for that matter. Times change, sometimes for the better."

Buxby gave a short laugh. "Sometimes."

A small boy ran ahead of his family, pelting down the dock, ignoring his parent's pleas to stop. He came to a halt before Emperor Norton, staring up at him with wide eyes.

"Greetings, young man," Joshua said. He extended a hand. "I am Emperor Norton the First, Sovereign of the United States and Protector of Mexico. I hereby welcome you to California."

The boy's father caught up with him and pulled him away. "Sorry if he's bothering you, Sir." He did a double take at Joshua's uniform.

"Not at all. Welcome to San Francisco, Sir."

As the two moved away, Buxby laughed again. "I bet he'll remember that the rest of his life."

"All part of my job," Joshua said.

* * *

Back in the city, various newspapers were putting out new posters. The river boat arrived from Sacramento with its Pony Express dispatches. Envelopes stuffed with messages on tissue paper went out to the various journals; editors scanned the tiny, crabbed copy from eastern correspondents and tried to figure out what they meant to say. Then they composed brief versions for the public posters and set out to create more coherent accounts for following editions of the papers. As a result, no one really understood what was going on. Nevertheless, crowds gathered in the streets, scanning posters or buying papers.

Buxby returned to his office, while Joshua made his way from one newspaper to another, gathering what information he could. He had to remind himself the news was still at least ten days behind; what seemed to be happening now had already occurred, like the arrival of light from a distant star. He remembered tomorrow was Friday, and he'd promised to show Sophia around Chinatown. Perhaps she would take his mind off these other matters.

* * *

Joshua called on Sophia late the next morning, but only after he had been handed another worry. This took the form of a written note from Marina. It came in a faintly scented envelope sealed with wax. It said,

Joshua,

Today some men called upon me, representing themselves as attorneys. They would not tell me who has hired them. They asked many questions about yourself, which I was unwilling or unable to answer. I am concerned about you. I wish you would visit me as soon as possible, as I may be leaving the city soon to travel East. Should I come to your rooming house? That might be more private.

Marina

He wondered why she would be traveling East. He did not concern himself about attorneys, since he had dealt with them many times before. But he should like to see Marina at least once before she left. He dashed off a note to her asking her to come to his room that evening. He paid his landlord's boy a dime to deliver it.

Sophia met him in her hotel lobby. She wore a dark brown coat, with no sign of jewelry or wealth. "Time for our adventure," she said. They walked the few blocks North to the edge of Chinatown.

"I'm afraid I don't know as much about Chinatown as you appear to think I do," he said. "I know only one person there at all well."

"And who might that be?"

"My physician. Dr. Luk."

"You have a *Chinese* doctor?" She sounded scandalized. But he didn't seem to notice.

"Yes, he's helped me a good deal. Perhaps you would like to meet him? If he's not too busy, that is. His office isn't far."

The streets of Chinatown were crowded as usual, crowded and noisy and full of arcane smells. They passed a butcher shop with live chickens in cages, and an herbalist with more strange aromas. Sophia was taking it all in. As they reached the building where Dr. Luk had his office, they heard a distant sound of shouts and angry words. They didn't stop to listen, but instead entered and climbed the stairs.

They found the doctor standing out on the landing, peering through a side window.

"Ah, my dear Emperor, and a lady. I fear you have chosen an unfortunate time to visit."

Sophia asked, "Why? What's going on?"

"I think a tong war. I'm not sure. The rabble from outside have been attacking our places of business, burning laundries and so on. Most unfortunate. The tongs do not wish to fight back; instead they fight between themselves. Stupid, I know, but there you are."

"I shall write a letter to the Governor, demanding he do something," Joshua said. "In fact, I shall issue a proclamation!"

"Perhaps that will help. In the meantime, it appears the riot is moving in this direction. I suggest we evacuate."

Sophia looked alarmed. "Is it safe to go out in the street?"

"Probably not." Dr. Luk gave a polite smile. "As I say, you chose an unfortunate time to visit."

"Forgive me, Doctor," Joshua held a hand in Sophia's direction. "I have neglected to introduce you. This is Miss Sophia Andrea Hull. And may I present Dr. Luk."

The doctor bowed. "An honor, Madam. Though I fear there is little time for formality." By now they could hear shouts and crashes rising from the street. "If you will follow me, please." He turned and plunged down the stairs without looking back to see if they complied. Sophia's skirts prevented her from moving as quickly, but she and Joshua descended as fast as possible. At the bottom of the stairwell, they found Dr. Luk holding a back door open. He had a lighted lantern. There were clatters and bangs from the front door, and somewhere the sound of breaking glass. "Quick, quick!" the doctor said.

The door shut behind them, and they found themselves on another staircase, leading down into darkness. Sophia followed the doctor, urged on by noises from above. Joshua came last. They found a dank basement lined with brick. Joshua had to remove his hat and bend over to avoid the ceiling. Dr. Luk moved across the room, which was cluttered with barrels and dusty boxes.

"This way." The doctor stopped at a large packing crate marked with Oriental characters. He lifted one corner, motioning for Joshua to help. Joshua took the opposite corner and they both lifted. Underneath was a dark hole, with five wooden steps leading downward.

"My god," Sophia said. "I'm not going down there!"

"It would be unwise to remain here," Dr. Luk said. There was another loud crash that sounded as if it came from directly above. Joshua went down the steps and held his hand up for Sophia. Looking white as a sheet, she took his hand and came down. Dr. Luk came last, lowering the packing crate.

The lantern light revealed a narrow tunnel, barely high enough to stand in; Joshua in fact had to bend over. It appeared to be carved from solid rock. There was a trickle of dirty water on the floor.

"Carved from sandstone," the doctor explained. "It goes about two blocks North. It was made by opium smugglers." He moved on down the tunnel.

"Are there rats?" Sophia spoke in nearly a whisper, as if afraid someone would hear.

"Only a few," Dr. Luk said. "Perfectly safe."

"Do opium smugglers still use it?" Joshua asked.

"Only a few."

By the time they emerged from the tunnel, Sophia decided she'd seen enough of Chinatown. "This has been more of an adventure than I bargained for," she said, brushing dust from a sleeve. "My dress is filthy."

"I was hoping we might sample a nice restaurant while we're here," Joshua suggested.

"Not today, I think. You may escort me back to my hotel, please."

They were in a warehouse used for storing wagons and carts. Horse and mule tackle hung from the ceiling. This end of the tunnel was not disguised; it opened into a small room within the warehouse, with a door locked on the inside. When Dr. Luk closed the door behind them, the latch snapped shut.

"Will the rioters damage your office?" Joshua asked.

"I don't think so. They have no quarrel with me. But it

is best to avoid the neighborhood of riots. Probably I shall be treating some of the wounded later. Miss Hull, it has been an honor. I hope you will not judge us harshly because of this incident. Please come again on a more peaceful day."

Sophia only nodded in response. She turned toward the door, and Joshua caught up with her. They found themselves on DuPont Street, near the business district.

"Perhaps I should summon a carriage," Joshua said.

"Never mind. It could take forever to find one. Come on, I can still walk, inconvenient though it be." She set off striding East, her heels clacking on the sidewalk boards. It occurred to Joshua that she might be out of sorts for some reason. He started to apologize.

"Please don't say another thing," she said. Then, "You do have some odd friends."

Joshua nodded. On thinking it over, he supposed she was right.

* * *

"Opium smugglers?" Marina asked that evening. Preoccupied as he was, Joshua had nearly forgotten about her promised visit. She had appeared shortly after he had returned from spending fifty cents on dinner at a nearby cafe. He'd had to spend American money since the place would no longer accept his script. "Is your doctor in that line of work?"

"Oh, no. Well, I assume he uses opium in his practice, so I suppose he must obtain it from someone. But Dr. Luk explained to me that the Chinese sell most of their contraband to white people. We're the ones who keep them in business." He had related the day's adventures to her at once. She listened with a quizzical expression.

"Miss Hull takes quite an interest in you. I wonder what she has in mind?"

Joshua shrugged. "Some people, especially ladies, wish to associate with royalty. No offense intended."

She smiled. "None taken. And you are indeed royalty."

Then her expression turned serious. "But about these gentlemen I mentioned in my note. From what they let slip, I gather they believe you have a concealed treasure somewhere. I suspect they are maneuvering to have you arrested on some pretext, so that your room can be searched. I only wish I knew who hired them."

Joshua gazed about the tiny room. "It shouldn't take them long to search. I fear they wouldn't find much. Except, of course, for the crown jewels."

She lifted an eyebrow. "Jewels? I wasn't aware you had any."

"Only alittle." He moved to the old wooden dresser by his bed. Opening the bottom drawer, he reached under some socks and linen to pull out a small tin box. He returned to Marina and popped open the lid. She looked in with a blank expression.

"You can hold them to the light if you wish," he said.

Marina took the box. "They almost look like real diamonds."

"But they *are* real." He watched as she took one between thumb and forefinger and held it so it was between her eye and the gaslight. "I brought them from South Africa. When I came here in forty-nine, I had some cash, and these few gems in a pouch around my neck. I couldn't bear to part with them. You see, whenever the legislature gets around to providing me with quarters suitable for my station, I plan to have them mounted in a golden crown. Of course, it would be worn only for affairs of state. In the meantime, I take them out now and then to cheer me up."

Marina stirred the contents of the box with a fingertip. "Your Highness, if these are indeed real, they're worth a fortune. You could buy a mansion on Nob Hill."

"Ah, but some things may not be bought or sold." He retrieved the box and replaced it. "Like the jewels of state."

"Perhaps you should put them in a safer place," she

said.

"Yes, you're probably right. I shall attend to that tomorrow. I do thank you for your warning."

* * *

Tomorrow brought more bad news, or at least rumors of bad news. Reports from the East caused only more confusion. Several Southern states had declared their independence. Near Sacramento, secessionist partisans robbed a stage coach of its gold. Joshua read every newspaper he could get his hands on, though they were often a day or two old, found in trash barrels or left on lunch counters. Bands of men were organizing to march East, or to sail by ship. General Fremont, lately of California, was heading for Missouri. Hundreds of newsmen had hundreds of guesses about what would happen next. Later that week, Joshua met Marina again at her hotel, this time to see her off. He rode with her in a horse car down Market Street, to the ferry boats.

"I wish you would remain here," he told her. "If only for your safety."

She shook her head. "There's no safety any more, not now." She had only one small valise with her, not even a steamer trunk. She'd left most of her clothes in storage at her rooming house. "And besides, I'm not making a living here. Back East, there are thousands of men in uniform, hungry for entertainment. I can sing for them, as well as dance. If that doesn't work out, I thought I might find employment at a hospital. There will be wounded to help—many wounded, I'm afraid."

The car's bell clanged several times, loud enough to drown out words. He said, "They say the war, if it comes, won't last more than a few days."

"They always say that. Don't they?" For a moment, she looked older than her years.

* * *

From the journal of Sophia Andrea Hull:

The Senator has been most sweet and considerate of late. Last night he presented me with a nice necklace of sapphire and garnets. And yet, he insisted on returning to Nevada this morning. It's all this commotion about civil unrest and secession and so forth. I do wish they'd have done with that nonsense. The Senator, in fact, uses the situation as an excuse to avoid speaking of marriage. I am not sure how much longer my patience will endure.

I related to the Senator my little sojourn with the Emperor in the underground of Chinatown. The Senator laughed and seemed to consider the whole affair some sort of joke. He may think I made the whole thing up, though he wouldn't say so. It's obvious the Emperor is involved with opium smugglers, and is only feigning madness as a way of covering up his true activities. Something must be done about him.

* * *

Joshua watched Marina board the ferry, and saw her wave to him from the deck as it steamed northward. He stood looking after it a long time. The boat would convey her to Sacramento, where she would board a stage bound for the East and far Missouri. He wondered when he would see her again, if ever. He chuckled a little, recalling their final conversation aboard the horse car.

"Nothing ever bothers you," she said. "Have you never lost your temper?"

"I have, at least once. It was over that cartoon."

"Which cartoon was that?"

"The one depicting me at the same free lunch counter as those two flea-ridden curs, Lazarus and Bummer. I'm sure you have seen it."

"Yes." She suppressed a smile. "I'm afraid I have."

"It was posted in the window of a shop front. I'm afraid I lost my good manners. Without thinking, I raised my stick and smashed the window. I'm afraid I should not have done that."

"No," she said, "but then, it *was* an awful cartoon." She burst into giggles. Then he did, as well.

He shook his head, remembering. He would remember Marina a long time.

* * *

A few days later, Sophia had occasion to meet with a certain off-duty police officer. They sat at opposite sides of a table in a small lunchroom not far from the Montgomery Block.

"Now, do you understand what I want done?" She stirred some sugar into her tea.

"Sure. I don't see no problems, Ma'am."

"You were recommended to me by those detectives I hired. They said, when you take a bribe you stay bribed. Is that true?"

In response, he shrugged and grinned, as if embarrassed. Sophia withdrew a small envelope from her reticule and pushed it across the table. He snatched it and shoved it inside his jacket, glancing quickly about.

"I want to search his room myself," she said. "I could have had those men do it, but I don't know how far to trust them. I am trusting you to bring me the key at once. Otherwise, I will have you exposed for corruption. Do you understand?"

He held onto his grin. "No need for that sort of talk, Ma'am. You can rely on me for sure. Anyway..." His expression changed to one of sincerity. "It's not like I'm the only fellow who takes a little extra now and then."

"No. In fact, I sometimes believe every single man in the city government is corrupt. Mark my words, it will be different when women get the vote." She glanced through the paneled window at the street. "Recently I was privileged to see a tunnel beneath the streets of Chinatown. The city we see by daylight is only the surface. There is a whole other city below street level, which we rarely see, hiding down below with the rats and sewer runoff. Do you understand what I am saying?"

He looked baffled. "No, Ma'am."

"Never mind." She shoved back her chair and arose to go. "Just bring me that key. You'll get the rest when you do."

* * *

Mr. Bannock didn't seem to mind Joshua hanging about his office. Most of the time, Joshua sat in a corner, watching and listening. The busy newspaper men accepted him as part of the furniture. What they did not realize was that he was becoming well informed. He was picking up news before anyone on the street.

Today, however, looked like a slow news day. Bannock sat behind his desk and lit a cigar.

"You say your friend Marina went East, did she?"

"Yes. She did promise to write as soon as she's able. What do you think of this Lincoln fellow?"

Bannock blew a smoke ring at the ceiling. "Your guess is as good as mine. Let's hope he's more competent than the last fellow in the White House."

"I should have given Marina a letter of introduction," Joshua mused. "I'm sure the President would be happy to receive a friend of the Emperor."

"No doubt, no doubt."

"When I was watching that ferry cross over the bay, an idea occurred to me. Why not construct a bridge over to Oakland? We could use Goat Island as a terminal point."

Bannock smiled and said nothing.

"Yes, the more I consider the matter, the better that idea sounds. I may compose a proclamation on the subject."

"Why not? We shall be happy to publish it. That should make front page news."

Joshua gave the floor a thud with his walking stick. "I believe I shall go home and do so at once."

He was only half way home when the policeman arrested him.

* * *

Sophia arrived at the rooming house on Commercial Street a short time later. She had the key firmly in hand. That copper had felt obliged to tell her all the trouble he'd gone to.

"I arrested him for vagrancy," he said. "A right and proper arrest. The fellow was indignant, but he didn't put up a fight, more's the pity. Then I takes him down to the magistrate, who tells me I can't charge him as vagrant because he's got two dollars and fifty cents on him, and a regular address with the rent paid up. Fifty cents a day. So I had to change the booking; they're holding him as a madman."

"Will he be sent to the asylum?" Sophia had asked in a bored tone.

The officer shrugged. "Dunno. He sees the judge tomorrow."

Sophia didn't much care whether the Emperor went to an asylum or not, as long as she could discover his secret. At this point, she had a strong hunch she was about to do that.

The Emperor's landlord answered to her knock. He was in shirtsleeves and gaiters. She suspected he'd just awakened from a nap.

"Something terrible has happened," she said. "Emperor Norton is under arrest. They are holding him in a jail cell. I have come over to pick up a few of his personal possessions. You do remember me, I trust? You know me for one of his closest friends."

The man scratched his head, apparently trying to absorb this information. "His room's locked," he said. "I'm not supposed to let nobody in."

"That's quite all right, you won't need to. I have the key."

A few minutes later, after some hemming and hawing on the landlord's part, she was turning the key in its lock.

The room was tiny and sparsely furnished. However, it was clean, with no sign of clutter or unnecessary items lying about. Of course, she did not expect to find Emperor Norton's treasure concealed in this room. She did hope to find some clue to its location. Perhaps a deed to a plot of land, or even a copy of his will. She was confident that if she searched thoroughly enough, something would turn up. She began by looking under the mattress.

The closet was next, with its few articles of clothing; she searched in every pocket. The small writing desk was next; there were a few scattered notes, but nothing making any sense. Something about abolishing the United States Congress. She saved the chest of drawers for last, working from the top drawer downward. There were a few coins, a clasp knife, pens and pencils. A couple of threadbare shirts, woolen socks and underwear. Finally, she came to the tin box in the bottom drawer.

Sophia pried off the lid and peered inside. She carried it over to the one window so as to see more clearly. Then she took one of the diamonds between thumb and forefinger, holding it to the light.

"Not a bad fake," she said aloud. "No doubt quartz." Of course, they could not be real; only a true madman would leave so many diamonds lying about like this. If they were actually real, Norton could sell one and buy a house. She shook her head and replaced the jewels where she'd found them. She was disappointed not to have found what she was searching for. She wondered if perhaps Norton really was a pauper after all. Then again, perhaps she had simply been looking in the wrong place. She examined the room to make sure nothing appeared disturbed. Then she went out, locking the door behind. The landlord was snoring in the parlor.

Chapter 5

Marina asked herself how she had come to this awful place. At the moment, the interior of this farm house did not appear terrible, but she had a feeling it would soon be full of horror. It had been commandeered for use as a field hospital. She had, in a manner of speaking, volunteered to remain and help.

She looked at the face of the young second lieutenant, the company surgeon here. He'd ordered all the furniture moved to the backyard, except for two tables for use in surgery. Now he fussed about, examining his instruments, now and then glancing out the open door or a side window. Two privates stood by, waiting for orders. All three wore clean white aprons.

She moved to look out the window for herself. In this early dawn she could see men moving in the distance, but couldn't tell their uniforms. The clothing of both sides looked so much alike, anyway. A lot of the rebels wore civilian dress.

"What is this place called?" she asked the surgeon.

He looked distracted, picked up a scalpel to test its edge on his thumb. "Wilson's Creek," he answered absently.

It was all happening so fast. Three days ago she had been at the theater in St. Joseph, singing and meeting important people. She had spoken to General Fremont. That was after the concert, at a private soirée.

"I understand you are newly arrived in Missouri," the general said. "I trust you find your stay a pleasant one?"

"I have been here for a week or so. After the stage ride from California, I never wanted to travel again. But I had thought to take the railroad back to Washington. I would truly like to see for myself what's going on there."

Fremont's smile was pure charm. "There's more going on here in Missouri than back East. Perhaps you should consider staying awhile."

"I have not quite decided yet. Do you think there will be more fighting in Missouri, Sir? I thought everything was under control here."

He sipped at his champagne. "Under control for the moment. As long as General Lyon doesn't go stirring up trouble again."

"Ah, yes. I've heard of him. Wasn't he responsible for the St. Louis massacre? That's where a lot of the trouble started."

Fremont stared across the room, as if thinking of something else. "The man's a fool," he said softly.

"I heard he once slaughtered some Pomo Indians back in California."

Fremont gave her a sharp glance. "You say you want to find out what's going on. Perhaps you should go talk to Lyon. I could arrange for you to ride out with a medical wagon."

* * *

That was how she had come to be here. She had not expected a battle. Fremont had ordered Lyon not to engage the enemy. Or so she'd heard. She had come out with the thought of entertaining the Union troops and perhaps meeting the General. By the time the medical wagon arrived, there were already troops on the move.

From the other side of the field, there was a thunderous roar. It was the first time she'd heard a cannon fired, except for occasional salutes out at the San Francisco Presidio. This was closer, and terrifying. They were firing live shot. In the distance, men were yelling.

For no reason, she thought of her friend Emperor Norton. She wondered that she could have ever thought him mad. What was happening here and now was madness. The sun had just cleared the horizon, throwing long stark shadows across the fields outside. Marina, being in the theater, had rarely seen the world this early in the morning. Last night she had slept for only three hours or so, fully dressed, in the ambulance. She had a sudden thought that perhaps this was all an ugly dream from which she would shortly awaken, yawn, and go back to sleep. If only it were so.

The lieutenant—she tried to recall his name, Grady or O'Grady, or perhaps Brady? —saw her arrive with the medical wagon the previous evening. He'd assumed she was a nurse, and began issuing orders, which she did her best to follow. She'd even helped to put up the hospital tent behind the farmhouse. Lieutenant Brady, if that was his name, seemed on a constant nervous edge. She did not believe he had slept at all.

Across the field, there was a rattle of musket fire, and more shouts. It was a short time later the first casualties arrived.

Later, she could recall only bits and pieces of that morning, bright but solitary images, with blank spaces between. There was the soldier who walked in by himself, clutching his bloody arm. She had cut off his jacket and got him to lie on a table. The man had made no sound at all. The surgeon showed her how to give chloroform, while he performed an amputation. It was done quickly, over with before she knew it. The two enlisted men got him off the table and into the other room before he was fully awake. Another took his place.

At first she was puzzled why some of the wounded were treated at once, and others not. Some the surgeon merely examined for a moment, then directed the stretcher bearers to carry out to the tent. Then she overheard his comment as he leaned over a young soldier and pulled open the boy's jacket. "Stomach wound. Put him out in the tent." She understood; there was nothing to be done for stomach wounds.

There was a lull in the fighting, judging by the lack of noise outside; yet the casualties kept coming. Marina glanced down once at her own white apron and realized it was soaked in blood. Her dress would not be much cleaner. She leaned over a grizzled sergeant who was thrashing on the table, only half conscious while she held him down. The surgeon's saw made a rasping sound on bone.

Then, at some point, a man in captain's uniform came through the door.

"Get ready to evacuate!" he ordered. "The army's pulling back to Springfield."

The lieutenant nodded, intent on the stitches he was putting in a severed arm stump.

"Who won the battle?" Marina asked. She surprised herself by speaking.

The captain shrugged. "Damned if I know, miss. Looks to me like nobody won."

"I was hoping I might meet General Lyon here."

He gave her a strange look. "Better hope you don't, Miss. He's dead." Then he turned and was out the door.

* * *

She found herself somehow back in Springfield. She could not quite remember getting there. She was looking out a parlor window at the busy street below; one of the medical officers had arranged for her to room with his wife, a citizen of Missouri and a Union sympathizer. She remembered that much. What was the woman's name? Oh yes, Amanda, that was it. Marina watched the traffic outside, the constant movement of army wagons and marching troops.

"Ready for some breakfast, Miss?" Marina turned at the voice of Amanda's maid, Julia. It was coming back to her. This place was so confusing. Julia was a slave, yet Amanda was for the Union. Missouri was a border state, half of one mind and half another.

"Where is your lady?" Marina asked. "I mean Amanda."

"Down at army headquarters, seeing to her husband. He's that busy these days, the missus hardly gets to see him.

She takes him a hot lunch every day, she does."

Marina decided she was hungry, though in some ways this fact astonished her. There had been times in the last few days when she thought she could never stand the sight of food again. She followed Julia to the dining room. Julia brought her some poached eggs and toast.

"Julia, has there been any news? What about Wilson's Creek? Who won the battle?"

Julia frowned, as if thinking. "Well, Miss, from what I hear, the rebels say they won the battle. But they're not advancing, that's what I hear. I guess the army is still running things. But then, I'm not the one to ask."

Marina had a feeling that Julia might be better informed than a lot of white people she worked for. "Who's running Springfield, with General Lyon gone?"

Julia shrugged and said she surely didn't know. Marina dropped her questions. "If Amanda returns, you may tell her I went to visit the hospital, after breakfast. Thank you Julia, that will be all."

Marina finished her breakfast in silence, then left the house. She could remember the hospital. The place had been worse than anything she could have dreamed in a nightmare. She could still remember the screams and moans. She knew she had been there a long time, trying to help, cleaning blood, bringing water to dying soldiers, carrying bandages, and other tasks she did not wish to recall. She wasn't sure how long she had been there, or how long it was since she had left. She thought she had been sleeping for a day or two. She had no trouble finding her way there; it was a commandeered warehouse on the edge of town. She steeled herself to the screams and moans that she expected. Yet when she arrived at the front door, it was oddly quiet. A Union corporal stood guard at the front door.

"May I enter? I am a nurse."

The soldier nodded. "Yes, Ma'am. I know. Go on in."

For a moment, she wondered when and how she had become a nurse. The words had come automatically to her lips, though she knew nothing of medicine. Inside, the light was dim. An army surgeon was moving from one bed to another, making notes in a thick book. He gave a strained smile when he saw her. "Back already, I see. I hope you had some rest."

She did not recognize the man. She glanced down the row of beds, or rather pallets. Most of them were simply mats on the floor. "Why are so many beds empty? It's so quiet in here."

He shook his head. "What did you expect? A lot of our casualties have died. They're all buried by now. What's left, the lucky ones, we've got on laudanum. The place is fairly under control, at least till the next battle. If you want to make yourself useful, why don't you go ask the sergeant what he wants you to do?"

* * *

She did that, and spent the rest of the day performing what chores the orderly directed. She left the place after nightfall, when the surgeon ordered her out. She meant to return to Amanda's house, not knowing where else to go, but she was distracted by music. Somewhere a man was singing.

She turned aside, following the sounds. The singing stopped, followed by polite applause. Marina strolled down one of the wider streets, to the front of what appeared to be a music hall.

She stood listening outside for awhile. The singer was followed by someone playing a fiddle tune, some country melody she didn't know. It occurred to her that she had only a little money left. Of course she wasn't being paid for her nursing duties. In fact, she remembered she had only a few clothes; what little luggage she had was somewhere back in St. Joseph. She had planned to spend only a day or two in Springfield. How long had she been here now—a week? Or was it two?

She made up her mind and entered the door of the hall. The place was filled mostly with soldiers, with a few women and some civilians. Heads turned to examine her as she walked down the aisle. It occurred to her they were noticing her bloody dress. She looked only at the fiddle player. He was a young corporal, little more than a boy. As she approached he glanced at her, but never stopped playing. She mounted the stage without a pause. She stood and studied the soldier's face as he played. When finally he came to the end of his piece, he looked at her and smiled.

"Do you know any Stephen Foster?" she asked. "How about Hard Times?"

"Yes, Miss. I surely do." And he struck a chord and began to play. She waited till he had gone through the first bar, then faced the audience and lifted up her voice.

> *Let us pause in life's pleasures and count its many tears,*
> *While we all sup sorrow with the poor…*

If someone had asked Marina how she could sing like this, she would have had no answer. She had not the least idea, herself. Her voice took flight, independent of her weary body, free of pain or fear or even hunger. Her song floated on across the room, above the audience, through the air, the air that was her breath, that issued from her throat, that moved across the crowd of men and women, to be breathed in again by their lungs and hearts and souls.

> *Many days you have lingered around my cabin door;*
> *Oh hard times come again no more.*

When she came to the last verse and ceased to sing, the

corporal put down his fiddle. For a moment there was silence in the room. Marina had a sudden fear that her audience had no liking for her. Then someone in the back of the room began to clap. In another moment every man and woman in the room were on their feet applauding. There were shouts of *"encore!"*

Marina looked at the soldier with the fiddle. "What's your name?"

"Randall, Miss."

"I am Marina. Do you know more songs of Mr. Foster?"

"Surely, Ma'am. I know them all."

"Beautiful Dreamer, then."

And so she went on to sing six or seven songs—she soon lost count. Randall was a fine violinist and a perfect accompaniment. He sensed exactly how to follow her pitch and tempo, as if they had rehearsed together for weeks. They ended finally with that Gold Rush song, *O' Suzanna.*

After each song, there had been coins tossed onto the stage. An officer wearing a colonel's brocade came up and formally thanked Marina for a fine recital. He gave her a low bow, then turned to the audience.

"All right, men. We have had a fine evening's entertainment. Let's hope this lady can come back again. But we're all up for early muster tomorrow, so let's all get back to camp. Look sharp now!"

Soon the audience had all filed out, the civilians leaving last. The corporal was putting his fiddle in its case.

"All this money on the stage, Miss. It's properly yours. I'll pick it up for you."

"You may pick it up, but you must keep half. If not for your fiddle I would not have been able to sing."

He chuckled and began scooping coins into his cap. There were a few gold coins, and a number of silver. They overflowed his cap.

"You'll have to take care of my half for me, Miss. I

might be going into battle tomorrow, I couldn't carry all that. You can count it later. Give me my half some other time."

She poured the coins into her reticule. "How will I find you again, Randall?"

He shrugged. "Just ask for Randall the fiddler. Everybody in the regiment knows me."

"Will you walk me back to the house where I'm staying?"

"An honor, Miss Marina."

On the way, she asked him where he was from.

"Born in Indiana," he said. "But my pa took me out to California during the Rush. He left my ma and two sisters back home. He was thinking of digging up enough gold to pay for their passage West. But then he up and died of typhus. So I've been working in a sawmill up in Columbia. Until the war got started."

"Funny how many folks I've met from California, here in Missouri. I suppose you know Fremont was military governor of California for awhile. Now he's the same thing here. General Lyon was from there, too. Did you volunteer for the army, Randall?"

He grinned. "Sure did. I was that weary of working in the sawmill. Maybe after the war I can get a passage back to Indiana. I miss my folks."

"How many battles have you been in, Randall?"

"None so far. I was in the reserve force at Wilson's Creek, but we never got called up. I guess next time I won't be so lucky."

She felt a chill, as if something dark had passed overhead.

"Will you be at the music hall again tomorrow, Randall?"

Again the wide grin. "Count on it, Miss. Unless I have to fight, that is."

"Please call me Marina."

* * *

Next day, she went down to meet the owner of the music hall. This was a large, stout person named Orville. He was friendly enough, and managed in a few minutes of conversation to relate most of his life story, apparently taking it for granted that she would be interested. He had worked as a carnival barker and traveling snake oil salesman, among other occupations. Now he was doing well in Entertainment, especially since he didn't need to pay most of his performers.

Orville had heard her performance the evening before, and was eager for her return. In half an hour of negotiation— during which she made sure he got several good looks at her ankles—he finally agreed to pay her one dollar for each performance, plus was what tossed on the stage. Then she insisted he pay Randall as well, if he were able to show up. Orville balked at that idea, so she shrugged and got up to leave. Orville relented.

There were no battles that day, at least that she heard about. She thought of going back to the hospital, but decided she needed some time away from that place. She told herself she would return if really needed. Then she tried not to think about it.

That evening, as arranged, she met Randall at the back door of the music hall. He was cheerful and looked rested, though he said he'd spent most of the day marching in formation and practicing with the bayonet. "Music always perks me up." They were to be the second attraction that night, after an amateur minstrel skit.

The house was packed. There were soldiers and civilians standing around the sides of the room. Orville approached them, mopping his brow with a bandanna.

"Word gets around. This is a small town, they don't get many high-toned acts around here. Leastways not since the Shakespeare company last year. You're becoming famous, Miss. They're calling you another Lotta Crabtree."

She laughed. "There's only one Lotta. Let's go make music, Randall." A sudden thought occurred to her. "Randall, can you sing?"

He gave a solemn nod. "Reckon so, Miss Marina. Or so I'm told. I'm a tenor. I do know a few songs."

And so their duet was born. After her first two songs, with Randall's accompaniment, he put down the fiddle and they launched into an unrehearsed duet of *Beautiful Dreamer,* at first simply in alternating verses, and finishing together, their two voices forming a perfect chord. He had one of the purest tenor voices she had ever heard.

The audience went wild. She told herself they were hungry for any break from the terror and tedium of warfare, that they would have applauded swine squealing. And yet she knew as well that she and Randall were giving them a truly "high-toned" performance, one that would have done credit to New York or Philadelphia. She felt an upwelling of some new power within her, which she did not understand, nor care to.

They performed for another hour, mostly the same songs they had done on the previous evening. They did not try another duet, but the audience seemed more than satisfied. This evening there were more gold coins to be scooped up.

Afterward, he again walked her home. She insisted he take some money, besides the one dollar that Orville paid. She pressed upon him some gold, so he wouldn't need to carry so many coins. There was a small park, or town square, on the way, with a single gas light. She invited him to sit a moment on a bench. He waited till she was seated, then sat as far away as possible. She laughed and moved closer.

"Did you ever hear of the Emperor?" she asked. "The Emperor of the United States?"

"Oh. Do you mean that fellow Emperor Norton? Sure, I heard of him. I even saw him once, when I made a trip to the city. He's crazy, isn't he?"

"Is he? He thinks there should be no war, specially

between brothers. Does that make him mad? The more I see in Missouri, the more I wonder who is insane and who is not. How long do you think this war will last, Randall?"

He looked serious. "They say not more than six months. The South can't hold out that long. My enlistment is only for a year."

She turned on the bench to face him directly. She felt a deep certainty that something inevitable was about to happen between them. "Randall, I want to continue making music with you. I want you to come with me after the war."

He stared at her, as if unable to think of a response. He swallowed. Then he gave a long, slow nod. She seized both his hands. "Come with me now. I don't want you to say anything, Randall. Just come with me, at once. But don't forget your fiddle."

* * *

Dearest Joshua,

I can't afford the Pony Express, so I suppose it will be three weeks or so before you read this. Of course there is no hurry. I am writing this only to ease my own mind, since you are the only friend in whom I can fully confide. I am still in Springfield. Many things have occurred since I came, too many to relate in a brief letter. I still volunteer a few hours a week at the hospital—a terrible place, but I am glad to help. I know the soldiers appreciate seeing me there. There have been no major battles that I know of in Missouri, but the army is constantly harassed by bushwhackers, rebels who wear no uniform and have no military discipline, but who skulk in the bushes and ambush our soldiers. Fremont has declared martial law, but so far that seems to have little effect.

I wonder how much of this news gets to California? Did you know that Fremont emancipated the slaves in this state, but Lincoln rescinded the order? It seems he is afraid of other border states turning southward. I wonder if this President truly knows what he is doing?

But I did not wish to go on so about the war. I only wish you could stop this madness by means of proclamation. What I really want to tell you is that lately I have been happier than ever before, despite the turmoil around me. I have met a young man who is in the army and who is a fine musician. We plan to travel together when his enlistment is up.

Marina put down her pen, wondering how much to put in this letter. It would hardly be seemly to tell him everything—how, that night after their first duet, she had led Randall to the horse barn behind Amanda's house, the building empty and unused since the animals had been pressed into military service. She could not tell Joshua of how they had climbed to the hayloft, she urging him on in whispers, as if anyone might have overheard. The moon shone bright and nearly full through the open door, bathing the two of them in light like milk. Somewhere below, a mouse skittered across the floor.

"Please undress," she told him. "I want you to undress first." He opened his mouth as if to object, then closed it and complied. He helped her remove her own clothing, which took a good deal longer. She spread an old horse blanket across the stiff hay bristles, then lay down in unspoken invitation.

That was a month ago. Since then they had performed together at the music hall two or three times each week, and several times at Randall's regimental camp. He had been a virgin, unlike herself. He was, after all, four years younger than she. They had made love—how many times? She had lost count, but thought it might be six. Once a week or so, he'd been absent, out on patrol; he told her he'd yet to fire a shot in anger. She had tried singing solo, but it was not the same. She knew she could sing the same songs, but not the same music, never again.

Marina looked out the window of her room in Amanda's house at the setting sun. For the moment she forget the letter she was writing. She hugged herself and began to laugh.

Chapter 6

Sophia was quite put out. She picked up her journal and began to write: *The Senator has been most irritating…* Then she threw her pen across the room and stamped her foot on the floor. She went to her window and stared at the street. She would have gone out, but it was one of those drizzling and foggy days typical of the city. She rang for her maid. The maid took an ungodly long time responding. Sophia wished she could own slaves as they did in the South. Perhaps, she thought, she would move to Louisiana if the rebels were to win this silly war.

"Took you long enough," she said when Vera finally showed up. "I must have rung for you half an hour ago."

"Yes, Ma'am. Sorry, Ma'am." Actually, it had been more like five minutes.

Sophia picked up her copy of the day's *Bulletin*. "Have you seen the front page today? This is ridiculous. I refer, of course, to this item about the Emperor."

"Well, Ma'am, I guess the war news is slow in coming, so they have to print something else."

"I wasn't asking for your opinion." Sophia was feeling more put out by the minute. She would definitely let Vera go, as soon as she could find someone to replace the woman.

"Well, Ma'am, I did see that item." Vera seemed oblivious of just how put out Sophia was. "It says the judge wouldn't send Emperor Norton to the mad house because he never did no harm to no one. The whole city was in an uproar about his being arrested and all. So now the Chief of Police ordered all the officers to salute the Emperor whenever he should pass by."

Sophia gave a deep sigh. She did not feel like correcting Vera's grammar today. "Vera. If it is not too much trouble, please be so good as to bring me a cup of hot tea and some buttered rolls. I believe I shall go out for a walk later, rain or no rain."

"Surely, Ma'am." Vera gave an awkward curtsy, turned and departed.

* * *

Sophia did get out later that day, with no particular destination in mind. She thought of strolling up Market Street, to peer in shop windows. The drizzle had stopped, but the air was chill. On the way, she noticed a new poster nailed to a fence.

Joshua Norton,
dei gratia Emperor of the United States
and Protector of Mexico
will lecture, one time only,
this evening, 8:00 pm
at the MECHANIC'S INSTITUTE
on The Economics of Slavery

There was more, but she didn't bother to read all of it. The date was for this evening. Sophia was aware that Norton was sometimes invited to lecture at public functions. From what she'd heard, he sounded quite rational. His subject was usually economics or Roman history. She smiled to herself to think of a bankrupt madman lecturing on economics. No doubt he had his public following. And Sophia had little doubt but what that Mary Ellen woman was somehow involved in this particular event.

"Why not?" she asked herself. She had nothing better to do, and there was a chance she might pick up some clue she'd missed as to the location of Norton's treasure.

So it was that Sophia arrived in a hired buggy promptly at 8:00 at the Mechanic's Institute. She had been here a few times in the past, either out of boredom or because Senator Shields had insisted on attending. This evening the place was as packed as she had ever seen it. She found a seat in the rear and settled in.

Sure enough, Mary Ellen gave the introduction; Sophia was grateful at least for brevity. Then Norton took the podium, looking impressive in his blue uniform and epaulets. He launched at once into his sermon.

"The institution of slavery has oppressed not only the Negro, but Southern White society..."

Sophia only half listened, paying more attention to studying the audience. During moments when she did tune in to what Norton was saying, he sounded quite sane, though she wasn't sure she believed him. His idea was that slavery had held back the South economically because all the industrious youth migrated North where they might find training and jobs. Thus, the only ship building port in the South was at Savannah. Why hire expensive, trained laborers when one can simply purchase slaves? Of course, slaves didn't know how to build ships. Or read, for that matter. Sophia shrugged. She supposed the argument was valid, but she found the subject boring.

What she found interesting was the manner in which Norton seemed to mesmerize his audience. They hung on his every word. She wondered how he did it. He had some form of charm, or an air of authority she did not quite comprehend. Everyone knew the man was supposedly a pauper, and yet he claimed importance. His audience, witnessing his assertion of authority, his self confidence, believed him and awarded him their own confidence.

Tomorrow, Norton would be out selling his worthless stock certificates to these same people, or trying to pass off his Imperial currency.

Before the talk was ended, she found the air stuffy and oppressive. She left early. She wondered at Norton's secret and how she might use it.

* * *

Several days later, a letter appeared in the *Alta California:*

Do not be fooled!

The Emperor is no pauper! Nor is he a madman. Anyone who witnessed his recent speech on "Economics and Slavery" at the Mechanic's Institute will attest to the latter statement. Emperor Joshua Norton I has a mind as sound as a dollar. He realizes that should he be exposed as Not a Lunatic, folks will begin to question what happened to those thousands of dollars he managed to conceal from the Bankruptcy Court. The mystery remains: Where has Emperor Norton hidden his treasure?

Signed, Respectfully,
Socrates

Sophia put down her copy of the paper with some satisfaction. She considered it a good letter. Her pen name of "Socrates" was a clever stroke, leading readers to assume it was written by a man. She expected the Emperor would be furious when he saw it. Perhaps he would compose another of his so-called proclamations. In any event, she thought this might put a crack in his façade. If he were to admit to being sane and rational, then he would be forced to stop his Imperial pretense. The alternative would be to claim insanity. He would be up a tree either way.

Sophia decided to wait a day or two before going to see the fellow. Then she would sympathize with him. She might even offer to help him dispose safely of his treasure. She picked up a vial of French perfume from her dressing table, another gift of the Senator. She liked its smell. She would like to be able to purchase more of the stuff.

* * *

Bannock, as usual, had scanned the competing papers, so he saw the letter before Joshua did. When the Emperor dropped in on his morning rounds, Bannock drew him into his office.

"Now, I don't want to upset you, Your Excellency. But you're bound to see this, or hear about it. There's a letter on the second page of the *Alta.*" He passed the paper across. Joshua read the notice with care, then went over it a second time. He folded the paper and placed it on Bannock's desk.

"Ah, well. There are always evil-minded detractors about. This cowardly bastard won't even use his real name. What is one to do?"

"You're not angry?"

"One must exercise Christian charity toward cowardly bastards. Speaking of which, I have been considering a proclamation to combine the world's major religions into one. What do you think?"

Bannock smiled. "That's a bit over my head, I'm afraid. Would you like to write a letter in response to this? It's always good for circulation, when we can get a war of letters going."

"Perhaps later. But that reminds me. You may remember Marina, our famous chanteuse, now residing in Missouri.. I have received a pleasant letter from her. Of course, the date is a month ago. It seems she is quite a success. She had planned to travel on to Washington, but now she means to remain awhile where she is. Her singing is much in demand, in Springfield and St. Joseph."

"That's wonderful. I shall make a note, for an item in the *Bulletin.* Perhaps you will allow me to read the letter."

"No, I think it's a bit personal. However, I may add that it appears Marina has discovered a beau. He is a violinist, and they perform together. She tells me they plan to travel when he is discharged."

"Why, that's even finer news. Discharged, you say? Then this fellow is in the army?"

"Yes, a corporal I understand. Perhaps I should write to

General Fremont and order his promotion."

"Couldn't do any harm." Buxby arose and scooped up some papers. "Now, if you'll excuse me, Your Excellency, I must get back to work."

When Joshua left the building he passed a blue-suited policeman. He was gratified at the man's formal salute.

* * *

Later that week, Sophia did meet with Joshua, but in circumstances she would not have expected. She had sent him a note requesting an appointment. He had responded with his own note, this with an address and time for the next afternoon, a Sunday. She did not recognize the address, but showed up at the designated place. It was a large house on Octavia Street; there were several other people entering the gate ahead of her. Sophia wondered if the Emperor had lured her into another lecture.

Then she saw the woman greeting new arrivals at the front door, and nearly turned back. It was that Mary Ellen person. Yet, Sophia's curiosity got the better of her. She forged ahead and acknowledged her host's greeting with a grim smile.

Joshua rose from an armchair when she entered the parlor. He made a sweeping bow.

"My good friend Miss Hull. I'm so happy you could make it." He was wearing the same resplendent though threadbare uniform she had last seen him in.

"The pleasure is mine." She allowed him to escort her to the chair he had been using. She tried not to think about fleas. She smiled.

The other guests appeared to be mostly well-heeled society types, about half a dozen ladies and the same number of gentlemen, seated on various couches, sofas and chairs. None of them paid any attention to Joshua. A colored maid was serving refreshments to those that wanted. The Emperor helped himself to tea and biscuits. Sophia settled back and took some time to survey the parlor and its furnishings. Of course she had no desire to socialize with this Mary Ellen person. And yet, judging by her home, the woman certainly knew how to make money. The mahogany mantelpiece had obviously come around the Horn, unless it was from the Philippines. Sophia decided to remain and hear her out. When everyone was settled in, Mary Ellen strode to the middle of the room and turned in a slow circle, looking each guest in the eye. Finally she spoke, in a firm voice that must have carried to the street.

"There is a new world coming! What was high will be made low, and the low made high! The crooked will be made straight!" She launched into a tirade, her audience listening rapt and still. The gist of it all, as Sophia understood, was that America was in the beginning of a revolution, that is a "revolving," where everything turns upside down. Mary Ellen's speech was laced with Biblical references, Shakespeare, and common slang, all delivered with a Nantucket twang. Sophia felt like leaping up and shouting *Hallelujah,* but she restrained herself. She kept waiting for the pitch for money, but it didn't come. The woman talked without pause for half an hour, and then abruptly stopped. She said, "Thank you all for coming today. Please stay and enjoy the refreshments. I'll be happy to answer questions."

There was no applause. No one got up to leave. The room broke up into small conversations in subdued tones that carried a sense of urgency and worry. Sophia looked to Norton. She approached him before anyone else had the chance.

"Perhaps you could explain the point of all this, Your Highness. I expected her to ask for donations. Why are all these people here?"

Joshua peered at her over the ferrule of his walking stick. "Underground railroad. Mary Ellen finds jobs for escaped slaves. A lot of them work as servants in good homes.

That's what draws folks to these little gatherings. They want to help, either by hiring the runaways or finding someone who will."

Sophia peered at Mary Ellen, who was in deep conversation with several others across the room. "And she does this, why? Out of purely unselfish, humanitarian motives?"

"For the most part. Then again, I've been told on good authority that some of the ex-slaves she helps have repaid her by listening in on their employer's talk. They bring Mary Ellen all sorts of business tips; what firms are prospering or about to go under, that sort of thing. She does quite well with her investments, I understand."

"I thought it would be something of the sort. She owns a string of laundries and boarding houses, does she not?"

"Yes, among other things. She's well connected. Knows everybody."

Sophia accepted a glass of port from the maid. "And you asked me to meet you here—why?"

Joshua smiled. "Not necessarily to hire a servant. As a matter of fact, it was she who suggested you might like to meet her. She mentioned she might be able to help with your difficulties with Senator Shields."

"*What?* How would she have got wind of that?" She had never discussed that problem with Joshua.

Joshua shrugged. "Servants will talk among themselves. Of course, I have no idea to what difficulties she is referring."

Something clicked in the back of Sophia's mind.

"Is it true what they say? About Mary Ellen being a Voodoo priestess?"

"Oh, yes, that's quite true." Joshua grinned. "She was an associate of Madame Laveau in New Orleans."

Chapter 7

In October, the telegraph line finally saw completion, running all the way from St. Joseph to Sacramento, with a relay line running under the bay to San Francisco. The last Pony Express rider dismounted and drew his final pay. The service had been losing money, anyway. The lean, daring riders were replaced by men wearing sleeve garters and eye shades, tapping away all day and night in the back rooms of the Pacific Telegraph Company.

In Missouri, there were still no major battles, though news of the front further East was horrifying. Marina and Randall continued to perform, traveling about the state with the permission of Randall's officers. Several times they appeared before audiences that included General Fremont. Still, Randall had to report back to his unit in Springfield after each trip. He was assigned to put down his fiddle and pick up a rifle, leading his squad on patrol through the green and pleasant countryside, where leaves were turning to autumn brown. Elsewhere, there were stories of rebel bushwhackers lying in ambush, most often up near Kansas.

Marina, when she heard of the telegraph, took the first chance she found to send a telegram. She walked down to the office near the railroad station, where a clerk instructed her on how to fill out a telegraph form, printing in block letters and counting words. The fee was much cheaper than Pony Express. She felt happy, and happier still that she could share with someone half way across the continent. There was no doubt about which friend would receive her first wire message.

Dearest Emperor Norton stop I hope this finds you well stop Randall and I still happy stop Hope you get to meet him soon stop This my first telegram stop More important news to come but must first tell Randall love Marina stop

She took her time composing the message, with some help from the clerk. She had to remind herself that other people would read it; at least two telegraphers, and who knew how many clerks. Several times she crossed out what she had written and started over. With a glance at the clerk on the other side of the counter, she crumpled the rejects and stuffed them into a pocket, blushing. At last she handed across the final version, along with a few coins for the transmission fee. The clerk counted out the words and gave her change.

Marina turned to go. Her mind still struggled to grasp the fact that shortly her words would fly across the land at the speed of lightning. The Emperor would read them this very day. Truly, the future was coming at full gallop.

Meanwhile, there was still the war. Randall was busy this week with his military duties; it seemed the army could hardly spare him. Marina walked past the newspaper office, with the latest bulletins posted outside. There was something about McClellan using balloons to spy on the rebs. What next? she wondered. The future came with a rush.

She passed the Police Station, now manned by Union Army soldiers; Missouri was still under martial law. Outside that building were wanted posters, with the names of known bushwhackers, such as Frank and Jesse James. She hoped those men would stay away from Springfield.

Finally she came to her objective, the army hospital. She had come to know some of the patients, the men recuperating before they could be sent back to the war. Others did not stay long; the amputees sent home as soon as possible, others destined for the cemetery. She often stopped in just to sing a song or two *a capella,* unless someone could accompany with mouth organ or even banjo. The soldiers always cheered her. She stepped through the front door. Today it was cool inside, though not yet cold enough for the pot belly stove.

One of the white-coated doctors stepped over to her. "There's a man here been asking after you," he said.

"Oh?" she smiled, always glad of an admirer. The thought crossed her mind that, whoever this might be, she would tell the man about her telegram. "Which one is it?"

The doctor pointed with his bearded chin. "Down there on the end, at your left. He came in this morning."

The man's face was half covered by bandages. When she reached him, he turned his head and spoke. "Hello, Marina. I'm sure glad to see you."

"Randall," she said. She fell to her knees.

* * *

Later, she took the doctor aside, out on the hospital's front porch. She realized his beard made him look older, probably the main reason he wore it. He might have been about her own age.

"He's a lucky fellow," the doctor said. "His face isn't as bad as the bandages make it look. No doubt he'll have a scar, but he's not missing anything important, like an eye or a nose. I've seen much worse come in here. The only thing that worries us is the chest wound. It was a bayonet, you see. He has a broken rib, but it appears his lung was not punctured. He should recover fully, as long as septicemia doesn't set in. Of course, he did lose a great deal of blood, which is why he's so weak."

"A bayonet, you say? How frightful. He told me he doesn't remember much about what happened. His squad was ambushed."

"Indeed. Rebel bushwhackers. They killed five of his squad before being driven off. That was yesterday evening. It happened very fast, I hear. The survivors brought Randall in with a stretcher. He was not conscious."

"I'm glad I happened to come by here. We talked, but

then he said he was sleepy, so I left him. He did make one request of me. He asked me to bring his fiddle from the camp."

"I doubt he'll be able to play it for awhile, but I'm sure he will be happy to have it. Here, I'll write a note for you to take to his officer." He went back inside, to the small writing desk near the door, took out pen and ink, and scrawled a short note on foolscap. Marina thanked him and made her way back to her room. She did not answer her host's call for supper. She lay down fully dressed and stared at the ceiling.

* * *

Next morning, she begged a ride on an army supply wagon headed for the camp a mile or so outside of town. She showed her note to a young lieutenant, who went to Randall's tent and fetched the instrument for her. "He's a nice boy and a good soldier. We all like hearing his music in the evening. I shall pray for him."

She thanked him and turned away. But he stopped her a moment.

"Miss Marina. We enjoy your singing, as well. I hope you will return and sing some more." She nodded, unable to think of words. The lieutenant made a vague gesture toward the tents behind him. "These men—a lot of them are just boys, farm boys—they miss their mothers. I hope you will come back again."

She nodded, trying not to weep. She found her voice to say, "Yes. I promise." Then she turned away once more.

She chose to walk back to town, though she supposed she could have begged a ride. It was still early; she guessed it would not do to arrive at the hospital too soon, since Randall would want to sleep. By the time she reached town she had found her appetite.

Later that day, she did go to see Randall, and gave him the violin. He took it from the case, stroked it with his hands and then replaced it, making no attempt to play. He smiled at her from behind his bandages, but he seemed weaker.

The doctor said, "He's a bit feverish today, but that's to be expected. Part of the healing, you see."

She went to him every day for a week. Amanda's maid, Julia, was concerned, constantly urging Marina to eat when she wasn't hungry. "I can see y'all is hurtin' bad," she said one day. "How come y'all never cry?"

Marina stared. The question had never occurred to her. "I don't know, Julia. I guess maybe there's too much work to do."

Randall lingered for several days. On Sunday morning Marina went to church, though she did not make a habit of it. In the afternoon she went down to the hospital again. Randall's cot was empty. The doctor found her standing at its foot in silence, her face white. He took both her hands. "I brought some flowers," she said. "You could give them to someone else." The doctor started to speak. She looked in his eyes. "I won't weep. There's too much work to be done." Then she began to cry.

The doctor said, "He told me to give you his fiddle."

* * *

She did keep her promise to Randall's officer. A week later she went back to camp. The officers expected her, and they arranged a small recital in the evening. The first song she sang was *"Hard Times, Come Again No More."*

That was the last time she performed in Missouri. She continued working at the hospital, not knowing what else to do. Often, when alone, she would take out Randall's fiddle and caress it. She'd had a few violin lessons in the past, and Randall had allowed her to try it several times. She found she could play at least well enough to find the scales. One morning before breakfast, she arose, tuned the instrument, and began to play. She played *Hard Times,* slowly and, she thought, badly. When she turned she found Julia standing in the doorway. Julia began to clap.

It was at that moment that Marina knew what she must do.

Chapter 8

Sophia studied the waistcoat with intensity. It belonged to the Senator, or at least it had until she stole it from his steamer trunk. It was finely brocaded, with mother-of-pearl buttons, the sort of garment worn only by a man of wealth. He might not even miss it, since he possessed several others. She studied the object with such concentration she did not hear her maid enter.

"Miss Hull, please—"

Startled, she looked up. "Yes, what is it?"

"A message, Miss. I was told to hand it to you." She held out a small paper, folded and sealed with wax. Sophia recognized the seal at once. She snatched it and dismissed the maid. The note was, of course, from Mary Ellen, asking if she yet had what was required. For a moment she thought of sending a return message, then forgot it. She would go at once, in person. The moon would be full tonight.

* * *

The Journal of Sophia Andrea Hull:

Mary Ellen remains an enigma to me. I begin to think this city full of enigmas, or enigmatic persons. Least of all, I understand not why she has offered to assist me. I tried to pay her, but she refused. She claims that the ethics of Voodoo prohibit accepting payment for good works. I am told there are others who take donations, but she of course has no need, being already quite rich.

Why then does she wish to aid me in securing the heart of the Senator? I do not understand her explanations. She says the spirit Mama Legba has guided her to do this. I am not sure if I believe her. She says that my courtship of the Senator will have a certain effect on history, which she feels compelled to facilitate. I do not understand any of this.

Nevertheless, she has given me instruction and awakened me to the power of Voodoo. We are to perform a certain ritual, which Mary Ellen believes will secure the Senator in marriage. I have already performed one minor act; last week when the Senator was here, I slipped a few drops of my monthly blood into his coffee. This is to ensure that he will never be interested in other women. Next day I asked him directly, and he swore it true, that he loves no one but me.

Still, he claims he cannot yet marry, because of political reasons. When Mary Ellen and I complete this next ritual, his mind will change. Or so Mary Ellen assures me.

* * *

Bannock lit up a cigar and prepared to sally forth from his office in search of hard news. Of course, there was more than enough about the war to fill the front page. With the coming of the telegraph, something had changed. San Francisco felt less an independent, frontier city; it was connected directly to the world. Yet people still wanted local news, gossip about goings-on downtown and the latest political scandals. Sometimes Bannock felt nostalgia for the old Committee of Vigilance. Now, there was a fountainhead of local news and rumor! He was about to exit onto the street when he nearly collided with Emperor Norton.

The Emperor of the United States and Protector of Mexico looked less than regal this morning. His coat was unbuttoned, his beard uncombed and with a few drops of porridge stuck in it. His face was red and eyes bloodshot. Bannock's first thought was that the man had been drinking, but he could smell no alcohol.

"May I have a word with you, Sir? If you have a moment?"

"Of course," Bannock said. Norton was obviously

upset about something. "I was just going out. Why don't you walk with me?" They started down the sidewalk. Despite Norton's agitation, he seemed to have trouble finding words. At the corner he said abruptly, "Wait! You must see this." He shoved a paper into Bannock's hand. Bannock unfolded it. A telegram, from Missouri.

RANDALL DEAD STOP I RETURN TO OUR CITY AT ONCE STOP NEED YOUR HELP STOP MARINA

Bannock turned to stare at Norton. He could now see the man had been weeping. He tried to think of words of comfort.

"Will suffering never end?" Joshua said.

* * *

Sophia met Mary Ellen half a block down from the house on Octavia Street. Mary Ellen preferred that no one see Sophia entering her home, which suited Sophia well enough. However, they used Mary Ellen's buggy, driven by her own coachman. It was a fairly long drive to the cemetery on the hillside outside of town. By the time they reached it, night was falling. Mary Ellen dismissed the coachman after telling him to return in two hours.

They walked through the iron gate and up the hill. Fog rolled in and the air became chilly. Sophia pulled her fur wrap tight about her. Earlier, there had been some rain.

"Are you sure this is going to work?"

Mary Ellen put an arm about her shoulders to draw her close. "It's all the will of God, Miss Sophia. Have courage."

"I thought you only believed in the Voodoo spirits, not in God."

"Now, whoever told you that? The spirits serve the will of God, just like everyone else."

They trudged a narrow path up the hillside, till they came to an empty place between two tombstones. Darkness descended quickly. Mary Ellen withdrew a thick candle from her bag, placed it atop a headstone and struck a match. "I could use a dead man's hand instead of a candle, but that would be most powerful hoodoo. I don't think we need that. Now dig a little hole." She handed Sophia a garden spade. Sophia fell to her knees in the dirt and began scraping at the ground. Despite the dampness, the earth was hard. She had to stab at the earth with the spade, using it like a pick. It took a long time, but eventually she had scraped out a shallow depression.

"Do you have the coat?"

"Yes." Sophia took the waistcoat from under her own cloak. It was tightly rolled and tied with string. Mary Ellen went to her own knees and began to chant. Sophia didn't understand, but she recognized some of the words as French. Others she thought might be African. The chanting went on a long time. Sophia began to shiver. There was something about the chanting that made her afraid. She had never been sure of whether she believed in spirits or not, but now she was sure they hovered about her in the mist. For a moment she thought she saw them dancing there by candlelight. Finally, Mary Ellen stopped abruptly. "Now bury it!"

Sophia dropped the coat into the hole and scraped dirt on top of it. It disappeared in a few moments. Mary Ellen arose. "Better tamp it down with your feet." Sophia did as she was told. Mary Ellen took up the candle. "That's it. Let's go." They began making their way down the path. Sophia glanced back once, but saw nothing, for the darkness and mist. For a moment she could not believe what she had just done.

The buggy was waiting at the bottom of the hill. "Has it been two hours already?"

Mary Ellen glanced at her pocket watch. "Nearly three. We should go and have some brandy now."

* * *

Next day, Sophia awoke feeling giddy. Mary Ellen had told her the ritual was almost certain to make Senator Shields propose marriage. Of course, that would have to wait till he returned from his latest business trip. In the meantime, Sophia intended to amuse herself. When her maid brought the *Morning Call,* she glanced at the headlines. One item in particular caught her attention.

Prince Albert Dies
Victim of Typhoid Fever
Queen Victoria in Seclusion

This transcontinental telegraph was surely a wonder. San Francisco had the news as quickly as the East coast. The item gave her a wicked idea. She had not yet given up on Emperor Norton. If she could not wheedle his secret from him, perhaps she could shock it out.

After breakfast, she strolled down to the Wells Fargo telegraph office. She filled out a message form addressed to Joshua Norton, Emperor of the United States and Protector of Mexico, Commercial Street, San Francisco:

MY DEAREST EMPEROR NORTON STOP ALBERT DEAD STOP MUST HAVE NEW HUSBAND SOONEST STOP WILL YOU MARRY ME STOP QUEEN VICTORIA STOP

She chuckled as she handed the slip across the counter. "A little joke between the Emperor and I. He's a good friend of mine, you see." The clerk scanned the message without smiling and then took her money. Sophia left the office feeling good. That should get a rise out of the madman.

* * *

Next day Mr. Buxby dropped by Joshua's room. Being occupied in court, it had been nearly a month since he'd seen Norton. It took a while for Joshua to fill him in on the latest news. He spoke of Marina in a distant, puzzled manner, as if he were trying to unravel some mystery. Then, seeming to remember the telegram from the Queen, he pulled it from a pocket and handed it across. Buxby read it over twice, without smiling.

"Do you believe this is actually from Queen Victoria?"

"Why not? It's as logical as anything else. Yes, I choose to believe."

"What will you do, Joshua? Do you intend to accept?"

Joshua frowned. "Well, of course there will be the mandatory period of mourning. Normally a year, I take it. Naturally, we must obey the conventions. It's always possible something may change in that time. But I certainly intend to accept. This afternoon I shall send a return wire to Buckingham."

"Ah. Well, best of luck, Your Highness." He handed back the paper. "And what of Marina? You say she is returning to San Francisco?"

"Yes. Oh, I forgot to mention I received another wire from her the other day." He looked around on his dressing table, but could not seem to find it. "I'm afraid she has chosen a bad time of year to travel. It would be different had they not shut down the Butterfield Stage because of the war. There is snow in the mountain passes. She wired me from Carson City, where she may be stranded until the spring thaw."

"Oh, I hope not. It's better now than it used to be—there are switchbacks over the passes. Actual roads. If the weather holds off, she may be lucky enough to get a stage."

"I shall pray so. I wish I knew what she needs from me."

* * *

The Journal of Sophia Andrea Hull:

It has been two weeks since the ritual. I do believe it is working. The Senator was here for three days last week. I was able to steer the conversation in the direction of matrimony. Of course, this was after giving my four poster bed a thorough workout. He did not make an immediate commitment, but I feel he is coming around. He said something about waiting till the end of the war, but I

think that was a thin excuse, growing thinner by the day.
No one these days can open their mouth without
mentioning the war…

She had met the Emperor that morning, over tea. She found herself baffled at his attitude. She'd expected him to mention the wire from the Queen, but he seemed to have forgotten it until she asked him.

"Where did you hear of that?" He looked blank.

"I don't recall. I believe it was mentioned in one of the papers. Or perhaps it was just gossip."

Now he frowned. "I hope no one has been blabbing. I had hoped to keep our betrothal a secret."

"Then it's true? You plan to wed the Queen?"

"Yes, but not for a year at least. Of course, arrangements will have to be made."

She gave a sweet smile. "I suppose you shall have to disclose your net worth—your source of wealth and so on. These royals insist on that."

He shrugged. "I suppose. Hadn't thought about it. Do you think the stages will get through from Nevada before the spring?"

"They had better. Senator Shields wouldn't like taking the long way around." She sipped her tea, beginning to feel put out again.

Chapter 9

Marina felt a great weariness of the road. She felt weary of this stage stop, where she shared a tiny room with two other women. One was an older lady, en route to live with her grandson in Sonoma, the other a teenaged bride trying to join her husband in Sacramento. Marina gathered the girl's husband had somehow found enough money to buy his way out of military conscription. Marina was weary of both of them. She'd lost track of how many days she'd been waiting at this stage stop.

In theory, one could travel from St. Joseph to Placerville in twenty five days or less. But that would be running day and night, stopping only for meals and to change horses. Not many people did that; trying to sleep on a moving stage coach was not a feat to be mastered with ease. She had left Missouri a month and a half ago. Now she wanted to move on.

This morning another stage had pulled in. Already there were twenty or thirty passengers waiting at the station, more in town at the hotels. However, Marina discovered this latest stage had only two passengers, both of them soldiers. She found them in the dining room, sitting off by themselves, intent on their bowls of soup and bread. She sat down near them.

"Where are you men from?" she asked. She had long ago lost all shyness with strangers. Only after sitting did she realize that the older of the two, a sergeant, had a missing left arm. The other was a boy younger than Randall, with freckles and yellow hair. He looked up at her question; in his eyes she saw a sudden terror, which quickly faded. He looked back down at his soup.

"We're both from California, Ma'am," the sergeant replied. "We were fighting in Tennessee, till we both got mustered out. My name's Jedediah. You mustn't mind Edgar, here. He don't talk much since he got wounded in the head."

"Oh. I'm sorry. I'm Marina. Where are you bound for?"

He gave a weak smile. "As for me, I'm going back to my hardware store in Stockton. Edgar's pa has a farm up Napa way; that's where he'll be going. I was thinking I should take him up there before I go home."

Marina glanced at the boy, who didn't seem to be listening. "Yes, that might be a good idea. As for myself—" Just then the front door slammed open. A mule skinner appeared in the doorway.

"Road's open, folks! The trail crew just now come in. Stages are gonna start movin' soon as they're hitched!"

On an impulse, Marina reached out and stroked the boy's hair. He went on eating his soup.

"Do you mind if I share your stage? I get along with soldiers better than with old women and girls." Jedediah shrugged and got up from the table. They were on the move.

* * *

As it turned out, the soldiers were riding a Wells Fargo express stage. It was one of the first out the gate, while others were still loading and being hitched. There were also a couple of big freight wagons getting ready to move, drawn by multitudes of mules. There was a fourth passenger who climbed aboard the Wells Fargo at the last moment. He seemed to have no baggage, other than a satchel. He was a young, handsome fellow, with auburn hair and a thin mustache. He asked permission to sit next to Marina, the soldiers opposite. Then he grinned at the three of them.

"Here's to a fine journey." He pulled a silver flask from under his jacket and offered it to Marina first. She shook her head. Jedediah said, "None for Edgar here, it don't do well by him, but I don't mind." He accepted the flask and took a long swig, then passed it back.

"By your voice," Marina said, "I should think you a southern man."

"Which I must confess to," the fellow said. "Lately of Missouri. But I'm afraid I had no heart for the Southern cause. Two weeks of the military was enough for me. I deserted and headed West, begging your pardon, Ma'am."

She smiled. This boy had a way of speaking that could make anyone chuckle. "I have been in Missouri myself awhile, but it's time for me to return to San Francisco. Would you be heading for the gold country, then?"

He smiled back, eyes full of laughter. She envied him his laughter. "No, Ma'am. Already tried that. I'm afraid mining is not my cup of tea. It's quite hard work, you see. Nowadays I'm a reporter for the *Territorial Enterprise*. That ain't near as hard. I get to do a lot of work sitting down. Did you ever notice that folks who work sitting down get paid better than those who work standing up?"

She laughed in spite of herself. "My name is Marina."

He offered his hand to shake, as if she were a man. "Clemens is the name. Samuel Langhorne Clemens."

"That's quite a mouthful. May I inquire why you are bound for California, Mr. Clemens?"

"Reporter work. If you can call it work. I plan to make up some fanciful news stories and wire them back to the *Enterprise*. I was considering a travel story about the various saloons in San Francisco."

"That sounds like a job to be envied, Mr. Clemens. But do be careful, I pray."

"Careful is my middle name. Well, actually it's Langhorne. May I inquire in turn what brings you to abandon the fine state of Missouri and return to the fleshpots and cess pools of San Francisco?"

Her smile vanished. She responded without thinking, "My husband was killed in the war. There was no reason to remain." Only after hearing herself, did she realize that she considered Randall her husband, and always would. She turned to look out at the snow covered mesas that would lead to the great pass in the Sierra. She said, "I'm returning to the city to have our baby."

* * *

In the stagecoach, conversation ceased for a time. Even young Mr. Clemens seemed at a loss for words. Climbing the long hills toward the pass grew tedious and boring. As well as cold. With all the new inventions of the time, no one had yet thought of a way to heat a stagecoach. The passengers closed the shutters to keep out the draft, and huddled in blankets provided by Wells Fargo. Jedediah and Clemens shared more of the contents of his flask. The darkness and lack of view added to boredom. Now and then Marina lifted a corner of the shutter to peer outside, only to see unending snow. She wondered what it would be like riding with the driver; at least there would be a better view.

At length they came to a series of switchbacks, to carry them up a steep grade. At each corner the stage would come to a near halt, while the horses were turned. At least it was a change from the constant bumping. At one of these turns, Mr. Clemens glanced beneath the bench on which Marina was seated.

"I say, Miss Marina, do you play that instrument?"

Marina bent to pull out the violin case—Randall's fiddle. "Not well, I'm afraid. I did take some lessons when I was at music school. And Randall—my husband—let me try it a few times, but I have not practiced." She opened the case and withdrew the fiddle, tucked it beneath her chin. She recalled Randall usually played with the instrument against his shoulder, but she had never tried that. She plucked at the strings, surprised to find them still in tune. With a feeling of curiosity more than any other emotion, she picked up the bow and drew it across the strings, producing a good middle C. Abruptly she laughed, remembering something Randall had told her.

"Do you know the difference between a violinist and a fiddler?" Clemens shook his head. "A violinist holds the instrument under the chin, while a fiddler holds it against the shoulder. I suppose that makes me a violinist." She moved the bow again, beginning to play. She had given no thought to the tune, and only knew its name when she had begun: *Beautiful Dreamer.* She played slowly through two choruses and the reprise. When she put down her bow, both Clemens and Jedediah began to applaud. She smiled and turned to look at Edgar. He was staring back at her, with only a small fear in his eyes. After a moment he looked down at the floor again, as if shy.

Marina caressed the fiddle. She withdrew a silk kerchief from her sleeve, to polish the wood. This was Randall's fiddle, Randall's voice, still able to make music. An idea began to form in her mind. She would go on the stage again, playing fiddle and singing; she wondered if it might be possible to do both at once. She had not heard of anyone who could do that—perhaps if she held the instrument like a fiddler? She knew one thing for certain: Randall's voice was not yet silenced.

"Play us another tune, Ma'am?' Jedediah asked.

"Happy to." She wasn't ready yet to play anything fast. She played *Hard Times.* Samuel L. Clemens closed his eyes and shoved his hands deep into his pockets. He might have been lost in thought.

Chapter 10

Sophia had spent the afternoon at Mary Ellen's home, together with half a dozen other guests. If anyone asked, Mary Ellen would explain it was the weekly meeting of a small literary club. In reality, the guests were there to receive instruction in the religion of Voodoo, and to practice a few rituals. Sometimes there were two or three French speaking Creoles or black people present, but most of them were upper class white ladies, along with one or two men. The membership was not constant. Sometimes members disappeared for weeks, only to return without explanation. Sophia surmised they were off traveling somewhere.

When she returned to her room, she found a letter waiting. It was an odd looking envelope, battered and with several postal marks. She gathered it had been mailed from somewhere in Texas, by way of Mexico. She took the silver letter opener from her desk and slit open the side. The opener was a gift from Mr. Shields; he'd pointed out that it was made of Nevada silver. He was thinking of investing in some mines there.

The letter was unexpected.

Miss Hull,

I hope you will not think me impertinent by writing thusly. I have met you several times, being introduced by Mr. Shields. I believe I may number you among my few remaining friends in San Francisco. I'm afraid I can no longer count on Mr. Shields. I am planning to return to your city when this war is done with, which I expect will be no more than six months off. I expect to return to the practice of law, and to re-enter politics. I hope to be able to visit with you at that time, and am sending off this missive so that my reappearance shall not come as a complete surprise.

Perhaps, in the meantime, you might put in some good words for me with your friend Mr. Shields. If you could soften his opinion of me it would be a great help. Perhaps in the future we may evolve some sort of business alliance.

You may be curious about my situation since leaving your city. I have joined a Confederate martial unit called Perry's Texas Rangers—named after another Perry, I regret to say; not myself. We have had excellent success against the Union forces thus far, and expect to continue. The bluebellies suffer from poor leadership, and we have every expectation that Lincoln's government shall collapse before the year is out. I have been entertaining plans for what to do after. Of course I could remain in the South, and no doubt would have great success in politics once the Confederacy is free. However, I have always found the climate of San Francisco to be salubrious, and have resolved to return.

I hope you will have the kindness to respond and share with me your thoughts. I am eager to hear the latest gossip. If you should find it in your heart to do so, my address is below.

Very truly yours,
William S. Perry

The address at the bottom was in Tijuana, evidently some sort of postal relay station for getting mail between the North and South. She folded the letter with care and placed it in her dresser drawer. She remembered Perry well; he'd been forced to leave after that business about the duel with Bradley. So, he was making plans to return. She wondered if she should mention him to Shields. Shields himself, she knew, had no strong feelings about the war one way or the other. But he hoped to enter politics himself, and it would not be popular to express opinions supporting Perry—especially now that the man was with the Rangers. Still, the South might win, in which case Perry could make a powerful ally, especially if he became a judge again. Sophia decided to think about the matter. In the meantime, she had her own problems.

* * *

"I have my own problems," she remarked to the Emperor later that week. On this occasion, he had escorted her to a Chinese restaurant on the outskirts of the district; she had been curious about the kind of food these people consumed. She had been prepared to find it disgusting, but discovered it not quite that bad.

"The pork buns are delicious, aren't they?" Norton said, delicately sampling one. He closed his eyes and slowly chewed.

"Yes, they are good. But we were speaking of my problems. You see, I had hoped by now to extract a commitment from Mr. Shields. There seems to be one obstacle after another. I find myself in a quandary."

"Isn't Mr. Shields still married?"

"Yes." She gazed out the window at the crowded street. "That's part of my problem. In a manner of speaking David is still married, if one might call it a true marriage. He has often expressed his intention to divorce; then again, the woman is ill and may not live long. I have discussed with Mary Ellen..." She broke off and looked at the table.

"Yes?" Joshua managed to look quizzical while putting some noodles in his mouth.

"Oh well, I suppose it doesn't matter if I tell you. As you must be aware, Mary Ellen is a priestess and practitioner of the art of Voodoo."

"I had heard some talk of that, yes."

"Well. I must admit the thought had crossed my mind...I mean to say, I put it directly to Mary Ellen. I asked if she might use her powers to cast a spell and hasten the demise of Mr. Shields' wife."

Joshua raised his bushy eyebrows. "Really. And what was the lady's response?"

"Mary Ellen said she could easily accomplish such a feat, and might do so in certain cases, but she would not this time, because it is against the philosophy of her religion. Such spells might be used for self defense, but otherwise Voodoo is meant to bring about only health and prosperity, and not for selfish ends. Can you imagine such a thing?" She sniffed.

The Emperor nodded. "Mary Ellen is a person of high ethical standards. I wonder if Voodoo might be included in our universal world religion to come? Oh, by the bye, did I tell you I received a wire yesterday from Miss Marina? She was in Placerville. She should arrive back in the city tomorrow or the day after."

"No." She tried to sound pleased. "I had no idea. It will be charming to see her again."

"Indeed. I'm sure she will have stories to tell."

Part II

Some years later

Chapter 11

The Journal of Sophia Andrea Hull:

Well, Dear Diary—at last Mr. Shields' wife Mary has passed on to her reward in heaven. I was beginning to fear she might live forever. Perhaps I helped her along with some of my hoodoo rites; but of course I never mentioned these to Mary Ellen. She and I have been on the outs of late; I think she finds me beneath her station. So be it, I no longer need that witch. Mr. Shields has almost certainly made a commitment to marriage. Of course, there must be a proper period of mourning, for the sake of appearances. After all, there is politics to consider, though I must say I do not fathom how he can be a Senator from California and spend so much time in Nevada. Not that I have reason to complain. He is making a whopping great fortune in silver, what with lending funds to mines and then foreclosing. Mr. Shields is truly brilliant, I must admit. For some reason, he refuses to take a liking to Judge Perry. I should have thought that silly war was behind us by now. Personally, I find the judge's advice

invaluable, and I find him a staunch ally...
* * *

As Sophia inscribed her private thoughts to paper, Joshua strolled down Montgomery Street, carrying out his public obligations of inspecting the sidewalks and street lights. The city was changing; when he had first arrived back in forty-nine there had been neither lights nor boardwalks. So many changes, and yet his own reign as Emperor was a beacon of steadiness and security. He turned in to the door of the *Evening Bulletin* for his weekly visit with Mr. Bannock.

Bannock had his hands full of proof sheets, and was busy at the moment shouting at a couple of hangdog reporters. Joshua paused near the doorway to watch and listen with interest. When Bannock finished his tirade, he turned about, red-faced and out of breath.

"Oh, it's you, Your Majesty. Thought I heard someone come in. Please forgive my temper."

"Not at all." Joshua slapped his walking stick against his palm. "I have been known to have one or two of those myself. Tantrums, I mean. I thought it a fine performance."

Bannock moved toward his private office, Joshua following. "It's these young reporters we have to hire lately. Barely know how to spell. Don't mind me, Emperor. What's on your mind today?"

"Nothing special. I was thinking of going up to Sacramento next week to inspect the Capitol. The trip is less arduous by rail than it was in the old days by boat. Do you know they still have not installed gas lights in front of the Capitol building? I may issue a decree."

"That couldn't hurt. Be sure you bring back a full report."

"Oh, and I suppose you have heard Marina's theater is opening a new variety show this weekend?"

Bannock pulled a sheet of paper from his desk and held it up. "Full page notice, to be run in tomorrow's paper. That lady is a true success story."

"In truth. I have some free tickets, if you should like to see the show."

Bannock shook his head and picked up a half-burned cigar. "No time, I'm afraid. But you must drop in and tell me about it."

"Oh, I shall. Indeed I shall."

* * *

Marina, in her parlor, was also trying out her shouting voice: *"Heather Maria Randall!* Get in here this moment!"

Heather appeared, doing her best to look contrite. Marina knew the look well. "I have told you a thousand times not to leave your things scattered about! Pick up your shawl, and go put on your Sunday dress. Our guests will be here any minute."

"Yes, Ma'am." Heather did as she was bid. Marina turned to look at Gladys, her maid. Gladys had been with her some time now. She had originally arrived in the city by way of the underground railroad. "I suppose you think I'm too hard on that girl."

"No, Ma'am. Not at all." She spun on her heel and went back toward the kitchen. *"Huh!"* Marina said to herself, having no one else to talk to.

A bit later, the front bell rang and Gladys opened the door to admit two guests. By the time they were seated in the parlor, Gladys had brought in the tea.

"Lovely home," the woman said. "And such a grand view. Oh, forgive me. I told you I would bring a gentleman acquaintance, but I don't know if you have met. May I introduce my good friend Joaquin Miller. And this of course is Marina Randall."

Joaquin rose to deliver a deep bow. "Delighted. I have long looked forward to this day."

Marina smiled, taking his measure. He appeared a tall, dashing man with long hair and beard, wearing some sort of leather hunting jacket. He exuded charm as an orchid does its scent. Marina was delighted, but knew better than to put any trust in him.

"I'm so happy we could all be friends," Marina said. Just then Heather came in, wearing her Sunday frock, face well scrubbed and curls arranged. "And this is my daughter Heather. She will soon be fourteen." Heather curtsied and took her seat near Marina. She stared at Joaquin.

"Is Heather as talented as her mother?"

Marina reached for Heather's hand. "She does sing well. But I fear her enthusiasm lies more in Ina's field. Ah, but please forgive me in turn. I have introduced my daughter, but neglected to introduce you both to her. She has, of course, heard of you, and has looked forward to meeting you. Heather, this is Mr. Joaquin Miller and Miss Ina Coolbrith. They are both poets."

Joaquin said, "Ina is the poet. I am but a scribbler."

"False modesty," Ina said. Then, to Marina, "I have followed your career from the beginning. I used to go to the music hall to hear you sing, before the war. We were all such innocents in those days. The war changed so much."

"As well as the telegraph and railroad," Joaquin said. "And the Homestead Act. More and more Easterners moving West. The world grows smaller."

"My mother is a great singer," Heather put in, relevant of nothing.

"Indeed she is," Ina said. "When your mother returned to California, she created a sensation. The public took her to heart, as a war widow, bearing the child of a man who had made the supreme sacrifice. She appeared on stage playing his violin and singing his songs, and the audience went wild." Ina looked at Marina. "I do not sing with my voice, so I attempt to sing with words on paper. I fear I rarely succeed."

"I want to be a writer," Heather said.

"And why not?" Ina glanced at Marina. "I'm happy to

see your child speaks for herself. So many these days have been hushed up." Then, turning back to Heather, "What sort of writer do you want to be? A poet perhaps?"

Heather gave a quick shake to her head. "No, Miss. I want to be a journalist. I want to travel around the world and report on things. 'Specially in places where there are wars."

"Traveling sounds pleasant. I don't know about the wars. I'm a journalist myself, you know, as well as a poet. But I'm afraid I've not traveled much."

Joaquin looked at Marina. "And so now you have your own theater. Your success did not drive you to travel East like Miss Montez or Miss Crabtree. You stayed behind and made a go of it."

Marina gave a short laugh. "Sir, I think of California as *in front,* and New York as *behind.* If you look at a map, I'm sure you'll agree. But I'm afraid I'm not so much a singer now as a producer and manager. You are coming to our opening this weekend, I hope?"

"Wouldn't dare to miss it," Ina said.

Joaquin said, "I hear tell you are a friend of Emperor Norton's."

"Oh, yes. You hear correctly. Though I don't see him as often as I'd like these days—the theater business keeps me occupied. He does have a free pass to all my shows, so he does come by. Have you not met him? The Emperor is quite approachable by his subjects, unlike most other rulers." She spoke without a hint of satire in her voice.

"I think we would both consider it an honor," Ina said. "Perhaps he will appear at the opening?"

"I'll make sure he does. Heather, please write out a note to the Emperor. In your best handwriting, please." Heather grinned, moved off to a writing desk in the corner and took up paper and pen.

"The future is bright," Joaquin said. "The war is behind us, and nothing more to fear. I look to the future."

"As do we all," Marina said.

* * *

Joshua arrived early at the theater. This evening he used a special ticket sent by Marina, which seated him in the first row. The house was packed, largely as a result of notices that promised a new and unusual act tonight, never before seen on the West coast. The gas lights on stage were lit. When the audience became relatively quiet, the curtain parted enough to allow Marina's entrance on stage.

"Ladies and gentleman!" Her operatic voice rang out. "Welcome to the Marina Theater! We have tonight a unique performance by an artist never before seen in this city! Later, I shall introduce him personally. But first, I wish to welcome our illustrious Norton I, Emperor of the United States! I give you his Majesty Emperor Norton!" Her white gloved hand pointed toward Joshua. Wearing his best uniform, Joshua rose, turned, and bowed. The audience gave him a standing ovation. In one of the boxes above the stage, he could make out the figures of Sophia Andrea Hull and Senator Shields. They were both applauding.

With this ritual completed, the show commenced. The opener was a combined juggling and acrobatic act to get the house warmed up. After that a singing duet came on stage, with several sentimental Irish ballads. They were a young man and woman, introduced as brother and sister. The audience seemed pleased. Joshua wondered if they were really related.

The important act of the evening was billed simply as Andrew the Great. He was a middle-aged man in coat and tails, with a young woman as his assistant. Andrew began by removing his stovepipe hat, only to discover a live rabbit inside. And another and another. The audience howled. He performed several other tricks, and finally announced he was tired of looking at his assistant because the audience paid more attention to her than to him. He ordered her into a small box. Once she was inside, he made several magical passes;

there was a puff of smoke. He opened the box and she had disappeared. There were a few more tricks, but this was clearly the highlight of his act. San Francisco had never seen anything like it. The grand finale was when he closed up the box, made some more passes, and had the girl reappear. Their performance was a sensation. Joshua knew Bannock was in the audience somewhere; this would be on the front page tomorrow.

There were several other acts, some comical, some refined. After the show, Joshua made his way backstage to keep his invitation to visit Marina.

Her office was small and crowded, but she had somehow made room for four people. Marina introduced Joshua to Ina and Joaquin.

"Did you like the show?" Marina asked.

"Indeed. Quite wonderful. Especially your Andrew the Great. Tell me, does he employ actual magic, or is some of it trickery?"

She laughed. "You can ask him yourself, Joshua. Some of us will be going to that new French restaurant in a bit. I do hope you will join us."

Joshua of course readily agreed.

"I noticed," Joaquin said, "that you are no longer styled *Protector of Mexico*. Perhaps Your Majesty could relieve my ignorance as to the reason."

Joshua gave a tug at his beard. "Maximilian was the reason. Mexico could not handle two Emperors. Besides, there is so much unrest down there I fear I can no longer take responsibility."

"Indeed. You must have enough on your mind with the United States."

"I do my best." He sighed. "I must admit I sometimes feel I have failed. I was unable to halt the war, even after I dissolved Congress and the political parties and dismissed Lincoln. The suffering weighs heavily on my soul."

"You mustn't take it personally," Ina said. "It was not Your Majesty that fired all those rifles and cannons."

"As you say. Do you suppose this French restaurant would like an endorsement from their Emperor?"

* * *

The gathering at the restaurant was small but jovial. All the performers were there, in good spirits, which a few glasses of cognac could only improve. Joshua was baffled by the menu, being unfamiliar with French; he finally settled on a small *poulet au vin*, recommended by Marina.

Joaquin kept the party going with witty remarks that seemed to roll from his tongue without effort. The dinner was nearly over, with dessert being served, when the head waiter approached Marina and whispered something in her ear. She nodded and arose from her chair.

"Please don't get up. It seems I have a telegram, which I must sign for. I'll be right back." She left the table.

"No doubt one of her numerous admirers," Joaquin said. "Someone at the theater must have sent the messenger over here."

"Telegrams are quite wonderful, aren't they?" Ina said.

After a few minutes, Marina had not returned, but the head waiter did. He leaned over Joshua's shoulder.

"Miss Marina requests you see her in the anteroom."

Now what? Joshua thought. Something was wrong. He excused himself and followed the waiter.

He found her sitting on a couch in a small waiting room. Her face was pale and drawn. Joshua thought she was about to weep, but was holding herself in check. She held out the telegram for him to read.

GREETINGS BELOVED MARINA STOP HAVE MISSED YOU LONG TIME STOP ARRIVE DAY AFTER TOMORROW FROM LOS ANGELES STOP HEAR YOU GREAT SUCCESS IN FRISCO STOP LOOK FORWARD TO RENEWING MARRIAGE STOP

LOVE SIMON

Joshua could not help but sneer. "This varlet, it seems, is unaware of my proclamation prohibiting use of the word Frisco, which has no grammatical justification." He glanced at Marina, who stared back at him. "Who is this person Simon?"

She opened her mouth, then closed it again. She appeared to have trouble getting words out. "He's my husband," she said. "I mean my legal husband. I have not seen him for a long time. I had hoped he was dead."

Chapter 12

Sophia Andrea Hull had just come from a private conference with Judge Perry, when she ran into Emperor Norton on Powell Street. It flashed through her mind that this person always turned up underfoot at the most inopportune moments. However, she greeted him with a show of warmth.

"Still inspecting the streets, Your Majesty?"

"Yes. I'm afraid the sweepers could be doing better. I hope you will take no offense, Madam, but you're looking a bit pale. Do I find you well?"

She fluttered her fan. Today was hot. "I am well, only a bit irritated. I have just come from an unsatisfactory legal consultation—about a personal matter."

"Ah. I seem to recall having been at one time involved with attorneys, myself. They cost me my fortune. But then I became Emperor, so it's of no matter now. Is there any way I might help?"

"You may walk with me a bit. Perhaps you might help me to calm myself." She had changed her mind about his company. She sometimes thought of the Emperor as something like a good-natured dog; she could say anything to him, and he would listen without casting judgment. Not that she entirely trusted this man; she would still guard her tongue. "How is your courtship with the Queen coming along?"

"Slowly, I'm afraid. But it progresses. Victoria still wires me on frequent occasions." Sophia had heard that other unknown persons had learned about the joke and took it upon themselves to send more telegrams from the Queen. To the Emperor they were no joke. Sophia still didn't quite know what to make of them, or him.

"However, now that I think of it," Joshua went on, "I might do well to consult my attorney friend Mr. Buxby, about another matter altogether. A situation seems to have arisen involving our mutual acquaintance, Mrs. Marina Randall."

This drew Sophia's attention. "Really? Is she in some legal trouble?"

"Oh no, not a bit of it. It's more of an ethical dilemma. But I shall say no more, lest I break a confidence."

"Of course. Mum's the word." Sophia made up her mind to nose around Marina's circle. One never knew when a scrap of information might prove useful.

> *Dear Diary,*
>
> *Today I consulted Judge Perry in his professional role as attorney at law. Come to think of it, isn't it odd that he is still called "Judge," though he has not held that position for years. I suppose it is like calling a man Captain or General after he is retired from the military. But that is neither here nor there. I told Mr. Perry I am not comfortable vis-à-vis my relations with Mr. Shields. We discussed the possibility of suing for Breach of Promise. Mr. Perry was not encouraging, but told me to wait; he said to see what the Senator will do next. He said there is still hope, but somehow I feel at a loose end.*
>
> *I have been thinking about why it is I have come to regard you, Dear Diary, as almost another person. It is because, in truth, I have no one else in whom to confide. I did confess to Mr. Perry a few of the Voodoo rituals undertaken toward Mr. Shields. But I could not reveal everything. There is no one else in the world to whom I might reveal all my thoughts, save my diary. Now I think of it, I am almost comfortable conversing with Emperor Norton. How odd. Still, even him I would not tell everything.*
>
> *I must look into this matter regarding Marina. My curiosity grows.*

* * *

Buxby, as a junior member of his firm, did not rate a

private office. He did, however, have a desk. Other people in the same room gave him curious glances when the Emperor showed up. Joshua sat smartly at attention, cradling in his lap his hand-carved walking stick and his new beaver hat with ostrich plumes. Both men spoke in low tones so as not to be overheard. For Joshua, a low tone was relative. Most of Buxby's coworkers could hear without straining to listen.

"...So there you have it," Joshua said. "This friend of mine, to remain nameless, finds herself in a quandary. She remarried in all innocence, believing her former husband deceased. Is she guilty of bigamy? There's the long and the short of it."

Joshua had provided enough details that Buxby had no need to guess at Marina's identity. He glanced at the other half dozen men in the room, who were pretending not to listen, and wagered that within a day or so Marina's predicament would be known all over town. He picked up a pencil and scrawled one word on a yellow pad: *Bigamy?* He had jotted down a few other words during Joshua's narration. One of them was *Simon.*

"I can think of at least one interesting historical precedent," he mused. "Andrew Jackson's wife—a case of accidental bigamy." Trying to keep his voice low, he leaned close and asked, "What is his full name? I mean this person Simon."

"Harker." Joshua spat the name. Across the room, a file clerk gave a start at the sound. "His name is Simon A. Harker." Buxby wrote down the name.

"And you say he is from Los Angeles?"

"No Sir, I did not. I said he is arriving by rail from that city. We do not know where he has been residing for the past several years."

"I see." Buxby toyed a moment with the pencil. "Very well, Your Majesty, I shall see what I can do. I will need to make some inquiries. If you should acquire any further information about this Simon Harker, please advise me as soon as possible. I am especially concerned with knowing his prior whereabouts. What I mean to say, where has he been living and what's he been doing all this time? You understand?"

"Certainly, Sir, I shall endeavor to find out." He made to rise. "I am happy to pay in advance for your services, if you will accept my personal scrip. It pays seven per cent interest, and—"

"Yes, yes." Buxby glanced about, hoping the senior partners were not paying attention. "That will be acceptable, Your Majesty, but you needn't pay us now; we can settle up later."

Joshua bowed, then turned and bowed again to the rest of the room, before taking his departure.

* * *

"There is something wrong," Heather said. Mr. Bannock leaned back in his swivel chair and gave her a long look.

"There is always something wrong somewhere, young lady. Perhaps you could be more specific."

"I'm afraid not. My Ma isn't talking. I guess she thinks it something I'm not supposed to know about. She's always assuming I'm too young to understand. She's making a big mistake. She may live to regret not telling me."

Mr. Bannock took this girl seriously. "And why is that? Why would she regret it?"

"Because if she just told me what the trouble is and asked me to keep it under my hat, I would. But if I can find out on my own, I will be under no such constraint. I might well compose some sort of notice for the *Bulletin*. Or the *Alta*. The papers are always on the lookout for some juicy scandal, 'specially about someone like the famous Marina."

Bannock did not smile. He took this girl seriously indeed. "Well, then, what leads you to believe there is somewhat amiss?"

"The way she's always writing notes and sending them off. I know she's had long talks with the Emperor. When I enter the room they stop talking, then they start discussing something trivial. There's something in the air. I can smell it."

"Well, then. If you should discover what it is, and compose a notice, I may well print it. We do appreciate a juicy scandal. Please let me know at once."

Heather frowned. "I was hoping you might have some idea what's going on. I know you talk to the Emperor."

Bannock shrugged and picked up a cigar. "No idea. But if I find out, I'll let you know."

* * *

Heather's sense of unrest grew, especially when her mother suggested she go and visit with Ina Coolbrith for a few days. Heather did not exactly refuse, nor did she at once pack her bags. She would leave when Marina insisted, but not before. Meanwhile, she found occasion to consult with Gladys one day in the kitchen.

"I'm sure I wouldn't have no idea what troubles your Ma," Gladys answered Heather's question. "Nor is it any of my business, nor yours either I guess. Nor would I say if I knew."

Heather shrugged. "Oh well, I s'pose it's nothing important. I'm sure you wouldn't know about it anyway." She moved as if to exit toward the dining room. The kitchen was redolent with the odor of a baking apple pie.

"Then again," Gladys said, "I does hear a little gossip now and then. Not that I would ever pass it on."

Heather paused on her way out. "Gossip, you say?"

"Well," Gladys was studying the surface of the coal stove, "I done heard somewheres that your Ma was 'spectin' a visitor. Some sort of unwelcome visitor, I heard. But that's only what I heard."

"Ah. An unwelcome visitor. Wonder who that might

be? Any ideas, Gladys?"

"No, Ma'am. Not a one. And dasn't you mention I said nothing."

"Thanks, Gladys."

* * *

That was on Monday. On Tuesday morning a messenger came to the door with a note for Marina. She tore it open and scanned it quickly.

"Any reply, Ma'am?"

She stared for a moment at the boy waiting on the stairs. Finally she dug a copper coin from her reticule and handed it to him. "Not now. But come back tomorrow at noon. I'll have a reply ready then."

"Yes Ma'am." He tipped his hat and departed. Marina turned and went to her parlor, where she seated herself at the writing desk. She withdrew a note paper and began addressing it to an attorney who had been recommended to her. She stopped half way through, crumpled the paper and threw it away. Then she spent several minutes staring into space. Coming to a decision, she stood and rang the bell for Gladys.

"I'm going out, Gladys. If there are any visitors, just tell them I'll return by supper time."

Gladys nodded. "And may we know where you're bound, Ma'am?"

Marina hesitated. "I suppose I can tell you. But don't mention it to anyone else. I'm going out to look for the Emperor."

"Yes Ma'am. I'll keep your supper warm."

Marina paused on her way out the door. She turned back. "Where's Heather, by the way?"

"In her room studying, I think."

But she wasn't. Heather was in fact in a nearby coat closet, hearing everything and watching through the partly open door. When Marina and Gladys were both gone she went to the writing desk in the parlor. She found the note easily.

The Honorable Simon A. Harker is desirous of an interview with Miss Marina, at her convenience. Please reply to Valencia Hotel.

Heather read the note twice. She also read the unfinished letter in the wastebasket. There was something wrong. "Miss Marina" had been her mother's stage name before Heather was born. Since then she had called herself Mrs. Randall. She wondered what conclusion to draw. Perhaps this Harker was someone who had known her in past years.

She made up her mind to see the Emperor herself.

Chapter 13

Sophia sat in Mary Ellen's parlor, studying the other woman's face. Growing older, the woman only seemed to increase in dignity and power. Her complexion was darker; Sophia had heard she was staining her skin with walnut oil. Sophia had no idea why, nor did she wish to ask. She knew Mr. Perry highly disapproved of Sophia speaking to this lady, but then he need not know everything.

Mary Ellen put down her cup of tea at last and looked across at Sophia. "You must know I do not deal in scandal, rumor, or gossip. Do you wish to tell me why you need this information?"

Sophia had prepared an answer. "You may not be aware that Miss Marina and I are very old and close friends. Of course neither of us wishes to advertise the fact, given our mutual notoriety. For some reason, she has been unwilling to confide her problem in me. This fact leads me to suspect she may be in a deal of trouble. I wish to discover her difficulty, so that I may find some way to be of assistance. On the other hand, if there is nothing I can do to help, I would know that as well."

Mary Ellen nodded. "I shall tell you what I think. I believe you wish to discover Miss Marina's secret so that you might gain some advantage. Perhaps it is a matter of blackmail. Do not make faces at me! More likely, you wish to put this lady somehow in your debt so that in the future you may reclaim a favor. This is how I read your own character. Be that as it may. I will fulfill your request." She paused for another sip of tea, watching Sophia over the cup rim. Sophia felt her own face turning red.

"You say the Emperor has gone to consult with this Mr. Buxby, the attorney. I am aware of him. I have several informants in the homes of people who work with him, though not in his own rooming house. Come back to me the day after tomorrow; I should have news by then."

Sophia, dismissed, arose. It occurred to her to wonder what favor Mary Ellen might one day choose to reclaim from herself.

* * *

Marina rode the Clay Street cable car down the hill to the commercial district. The car had already been running for two years, but she still wondered each time she boarded if the cable were about to break. She supposed this was another sign of progress, like the railroad and telegraph. She would have to get used to it; as long as she didn't have to travel by balloon.

The Emperor of the United States was not at home, nor did his landlord know of Norton's whereabouts. Marina decided to wait awhile in the parlor in hopes of his return. She sat for an hour with nothing to do but stare out the window; she had just decided to leave a note when she heard the front door open and close. She arose and turned, hoping it might be Norton. The light footsteps in the hall told her it wasn't a man. A moment later, Heather came in.

At sight of her mother, she halted as if she had run into a wall. At the same moment, both women opened their mouths to speak, probably something like *What are you doing here?* or words to that effect.

"You look tired," Marina said. "Perhaps you should come in and sit down. The landlord left a pitcher of water, if you would like some."

Heather sat near the window without a word. For a long moment she stared at her mother. Then she said, "Why don't you tell me what's going on?"

Marina stared out the window, then glanced at the front door. Heather thought she was about to turn and leave. Instead, she sat down on the other side of the room.

"What have you heard?" she said.

"Not much. It's more of a feeling I have. That

something evil is on its way. Something bad is coming. An unwelcome visitor."

Marina smiled with her lips, eyes sad. "Sometimes you remind me of your father. At times he used to speak of his feelings in that way. When he lay dying in hospital, he said he felt he was going on a journey, that he was waiting for his ticket agent. He warned me the entire nation was on a journey to somewhere we have never been, and there was no going back. But that's neither here nor there. I don't know what you have heard, or where, but I suppose you're bound to find out sooner or later. Life is a one way journey. I was married once before, several years before meeting Corporal Randall. I was young and foolish."

Heather remained still, waiting for her mother to continue, but she did not. They merely gazed at one another. Finally Marina's words sank in.

"The unwelcome visitor. He was your husband."

"He believes he still is, since there was no divorce. When I knew him, he was a gambler and a swindler. We dwelt in wedded bliss for about a year. He left town suddenly when he was caught dealing in counterfeit gold coins that contained more copper than gold. I don't know where he went after that. Truth to tell, I was relieved to see him gone. Now he turns up like a bad penny."

"He is the evil that comes our way."

Marina shrugged. "I don't know that he's much more evil than most. He never beat me, nor anyone else I know of. He never murdered or did armed robbery, that I know of. He never ordered a hundred men to face cannon fire. But neither has he committed an honest day's work in his life, that I know of."

"So what does he want with us now? After all this time?"

Marina smiled. "With you, I suppose nothing. I expect what he wants from me is money. He must have learned of my public success. Don't worry, I shan't invite him to stay. But it might be expensive to get rid of him."

"Why not just tell him to leave?"

Now Marina looked uncomfortable. She stared out the window again. "You're not famous yet, so you wouldn't understand. You see, my success depends on my reputation. The public is unforgiving. Lola Montez gets away with being outrageous, because that is what the public expects, or almost demands. What they expect and demand of me is to be of high moral and spiritual standards, the courageous war widow bravely raising a talented child."

Heather shook her head, as if trying to clear it. "But how does this fellow turning up change anything?"

"You don't see it, do you? Of course not. He could go to the papers, or even the courts. He could accuse me of bigamy. That would be a great scandal, a blight on the name of Marina Randall."

Heather stared at her, said nothing.

"Of course, I do have a defense. I could say Corporal Randall and I were never legally married. There's no proof of it, no record anywhere. But that would be an equally great scandal, wouldn't it?" Silently she began to weep, tears welling as if squeezed from a great depth. Heather crossed the room and embraced her mother.

* * *

Half an hour later, the Emperor returned. The two visitors had been about to give up and leave, when they heard the door slam and the familiar clump of boots on the stairs. Joshua entered with a thoughtful, distracted expression, but when he saw them he gave a broad smile.

"Good news! Mr. Hamilton is retiring!"

"And who might that be?" Marina asked.

"Ah." The thoughtful expression returned. "Forgive me, I had forgotten you wouldn't know. What a delight to find you here, and Miss Heather as well."

"She followed me here."

"I see. Well. Mr. Hamilton is a senior partner in Mr. Buxby's firm. This means that Mr. Buxby will at last be advancing. He becomes the most junior of the senior partners, with his own office lately vacated by Mr. Hamilton. Isn't that splendid news?"

"I suppose so. But I actually came to see you about another matter."

"Oh, yes. I suppose it must be the same business that I was lately discussing with Mr. Buxby." He glanced at Heather. "Naturally, you will wish a more private audience before we go into that."

"Never mind. Heather knows all about it now. She is by all means the nosiest young lady you will ever care to meet. Were you able to find anything out?"

Joshua took a seat nearby and laid his stick on the floor. He cleared his throat and loosened his tie, glancing again at Heather. "Well, then. In fact, Mr. Buxby was quite helpful in the matter of information about this Simon Harker person. He sent wires to the sheriffs of several different counties. It appears Mr. Harker is known in Los Angeles and also Monterey, having been arrested more than once for petty theft. More importantly, he was recently discharged from a Mexican prison after serving two years for cattle stealing. Aside from that, his main means of support is believed to be gambling."

"I cannot imagine Simon as a rustler."

"Oh, he didn't actually steal the cows himself. He would purchase them from Mexican rustlers, then sell them across the U.S. border. A lucrative trade, I'm told. His last contact with the law was more than a year ago, current whereabouts unknown."

"His current whereabouts is the Valencia Hotel in this city. I was hoping there might be an outstanding warrant."

"No such luck, I'm afraid. May I ask what you intend

to do?"

"I intend to meet Mr. Harker. Beyond that, I couldn't say. Thank you for your efforts in my behalf, Emperor. And be sure to thank Mr. Buxby. And to congratulate him." She got to her feet. "Heather and I shall be running along now."

"Let me know if I may be of further service. I shall accompany you as far as the cable stop. I was thinking of trying a new free lunch counter which I just heard about."

Marina took the hint. She opened her reticule. "Before we go, Your Highness, and lest I forget, I was hoping to invest in some more of your bonds, if you should happen to have any about. I think five dollars worth."

Joshua smiled again. "I am delighted to serve, Madame."

* * *

The Journal of Sophia Andrea Hull:

I was shocked today to learn the truth of Miss Marina's current trouble. Not that I have ever been fond of the woman. But I begin to appreciate what it means to be betrayed by a man, one whom a woman once trusted. I had thought to perhaps find some way to use her problem to my advantage. Perhaps I still may. Instead, I discover in myself an urge to offer sympathy and support. I shall do so tomorrow.

Sophia appeared at Marina's doorstep in the late morning, unannounced. She had not bothered to request an appointment, and half expected Marina to tell her maid she was indisposed. Instead, she was kept waiting only a few minutes in the anteroom. She found Marina alone in the parlor.

"I'm sorry there's no tea prepared," Marina said. "Your visit is a surprise. But if you could be patient for a few minutes—"

"I did not come for tea." Sophia sounded more

snappish than she had intended. "I mean, please don't bother. Is your daughter about? What's her name again—Heather, is it? An unusual name for a Christian."

"I have never claimed to be one of those. Heather is visiting Ina for a day or two. They have become quite good friends. To what do I owe the pleasure of this sudden visit, Miss Hull?"

Sophia, unbidden, seated herself on the edge of a chair. "I shall come to the point. I have heard about your problem with this Harker fellow."

At this, Marina's face paled. "Good God, have I made the papers already?"

"No, no. Not a bit of it. Perhaps with luck this business will never become news. No, I learned of it through confidential sources. Let's call it the grapevine."

"I see. The grapevine, is it? Then I can only wonder. May I ask, Miss Hull, how the matter concerns yourself?"

"It doesn't. Not really. It's only that I feel constrained to offer my sympathy and support, for what it may be worth."

Marina was silent a moment, taking that in. "Well, then. I thank you for your sympathy, but I really don't see what support you might offer. Not that I am in need of it."

"Perhaps not. But I am beginning to realize I myself am in a similar position. Although, it may be different for you. You at least have your profession and property. I might say your wealth, to be rude. I have nothing but my wits. If the Senator should turn me out, I know not what may become of me. Ah, listen to me. I did not come to reveal my own troubles, only to offer you help in yours. Please believe me, I speak true. Perhaps I should be on my way."

Marina had been watching Sophia's face, as if trying to read a book written in an unfamiliar language. She took a step closer and held out both hands. "You needn't rush off. I take no offense at anything you have said, Miss Hull. I'm sorry to hear of your own troubles. Please don't worry yourself about me. Let me know if I can help *you*."

Sophia turned to leave, tears starting in her eyes. She paused and gave Marina a strange look. "If you wish, I could enlist the aid of two or three gentlemen to give your problem a stern talking to."

Marina laughed. "Ruffians, you mean. I doubt that will be necessary, but I thank you for the offer. I'll be sure to let you know."

* * *

Two days after this conversation, Sophia was again feeling put out, this time *extremely* put out.

The Journal of Sophia Andrea Hull:

My worst fears are realized. For some time now, I have suspected something of the sort. Now Mary Ellen's spies have kindly provided me with the truth. More, I verified the fact with my own eyes. Senator Shields is keeping another woman. He is providing her with a room at the Baldwin, the very hotel where I used to live prior to meeting the Senator. Mary Ellen advised me he visits her on a regular schedule, Tuesday and Thursday afternoons. Yesterday I took a discreet position behind one of the large pillars in the lobby and observed him on the way in. I chose not to remain long enough to see how long he stayed. Most likely it was overnight.

This morning I went to the Senator's room in the Palace. I confronted him directly and inquired of his intentions. I fear we had quite a row. In the end, he averred that he has no intention of re-marrying, myself or anyone else. Further, he has ordered me to vacate my rooms in thirty days. He is cutting off my allowance at once.

He won't get away with it. I have a plan. First, I must have another consult with Judge Perry. The Senator is in for a surprise.

Chapter 14

Marina had not long to wait. She had chosen to meet Harker on neutral ground, a French restaurant on Montgomery Street. She ordered coffee with toast and jam. The waiter appeared disappointed, especially when she barely sipped the coffee and only nibbled at the toast. Twenty minutes after the appointed time, Harker showed up. She did not expect him to apologize for being late, nor did he. Without ceremony, he pulled out a chair opposite and seated himself.

"You haven't changed a bit, Marina."

"You have, Simon. You have lost weight. And the beard does not flatter your face. Have you been ill? I would hardly have recognized you."

"It's true, I have had some rough times. Your absence made it all the harder. I have often longed to see your face again."

"I'm not taking you back, Simon. I have my own life now. Is that what you wanted to know?"

He gave a theatrical sigh. "Ah, Marina. You were always good at being blunt. Perhaps you do not know how much I have changed. I have become an honest man. We were happy once—"

"And I was miserable once, but no more. Does your honesty include dealing in stolen cattle?"

He blinked. "Where did you hear that? Oh, never mind, I suppose you have your sources. If you will permit me to explain—"

"Won't be necessary, since I don't care. Why are you back in San Francisco, Simon? What was your plan? More counterfeit money?"

"Now, Marina, that's hardly fair. You're not giving me a chance. It's true I'm temporarily between occupations, and running short on cash…"

Marina picked up her cup, finished the coffee, and signaled the waiter for more. He brought over a fresh pot, with a second cup. "Will the gentleman be ordering dinner?"

"No, he won't," Marina said. "But he can have coffee and toast if he's hungry." The waiter departed. Simon looked at the toast for a moment, then snatched up a piece and wolfed it down. "How much do you want?" Marina asked.

He gave her a wide-eyed look. "You mean, how much toast, Marina?"

"No, I mean how much money? To go away again."

He took a sip of coffee, looking thoughtful. He lowered the cup and stared into it, as if reading tea leaves. "You were always a hard woman, Marina. By the way, how is your daughter, the love-child? What's her name, again?"

"If you speak that way, I shall empty this hot coffee over your head. Understand? How much money?"

Now he looked up and smiled brightly. "Well. Since you put it that way, I shall have to give the matter some thought. By the way, did you know I could have you arrested for adultery? It's against the law in this state. Not, of course, that I would actually do that."

"In any case, I believe there is a statute of limitations. But you think you could make trouble for me."

"All I'm asking is a fair shake. Look here, Marina. You're rich and I'm not. If you won't take me back, then you ought to divorce me. You should give me some sort of settlement."

"And for the divorce you would have to claim infidelity, which would ruin my reputation. You were always a card sharp, Simon. You seem to be holding all the cards."

He leaned back, picked up another piece of toast, and smiled, while spreading jam. He said nothing.

"Very well, I will give you an answer, but I will need a few days. I am not as rich as you seem to think. I will need to examine my assets. I will send you a note when I am ready."

"Fine by me, long as you don't wait too long. There's just one thing, though; there's the matter of my current hotel bill—I had travel expenses, that sort of thing..."

Without a word, she dropped a ten dollar banknote on the table as she got up to leave.

* * *

While Marina and Simon were conversing, Sophia was consulting not Judge Perry, but Mary Ellen. That lady was studying a spread of cards on her tea table.

"Something will need to be done about the railroad," she mused, "by someone."

"The railroad?" Sophia was baffled; the railroad had nothing to do with her problem, as far as she knew.

"Yes." Mary Ellen scanned the cards, one side to the other. "Everyone thought the Western Pacific would bring progress and civilization to the West. Instead, it has brought tyranny."

"Oh. Yes, the Senator was discussing that the other day. The miners don't like it much." Vaguely, she recalled what she had read in the *Chronicle* and the *Alta*. The railroad owned half the state of California, charging what rates they pleased of the farms and factories. It was the latest political issue, replacing slavery.

Mary Ellen leaned back and looked at Sophia. "A new kind of slavery," she said, "of the pocketbook. This time the railroad is not underground."

"More's the pity. What do the cards tell you, Mary Ellen?"

"Nothing I did not expect. You have a chance to prevail against the Senator, but nothing is certain. You must act quickly and with determination."

"Oh, I shall. I have already had a brief discussion with Mr. Perry. He agrees I have a chance."

Mary Ellen gave her a quizzical look. "What else did your judge say?"

Now Sophia felt uncomfortable, but she decided not to hold back. "He asked me if I had any samples of the Senator's handwriting. I mean, his signature."

"And did you?"

"Of course. I have every letter and note he ever sent me. I also have a piece of blank paper with his name signed at the bottom. It was for the bank, you see, to verify his signature. He was to bring it to the Bank of California, about a year ago. But he left it on his desk, so I kept it, thinking it might one day be useful. He'd forgotten all about it."

"Ah. Then perhaps I'd better not ask what Judge Perry intends it for. I see no other message in the cards for you."

* * *

The Emperor seldom played cards, but lately he had begun indulging in a few games of penny ante with Mr. Bannock. Usually Bannock had to stake Joshua, who agreed to play because it seemed to help the other man relax. Bannock had taken to remaining in his office well into the night, even after the pressmen had gone home.

"I guess I'm getting an ulcer," Bannock remarked, studying his hand. "Can't seem to keep anything down lately. Pass me that whisky, would you?" He took the bottle and poured himself a shot. "What news do you hear of that problem of your friend Marina?"

"You know about that, then?" Joshua studied his hand of cards. Bannock discarded one and drew another.

"Tales get about. Heather was in here a few days ago asking about it. She said she might write a notice for the paper."

"I hope it doesn't go that far."

Bannock shrugged. "I have no wish to harm your friend, but as I say, tales get about. I went so far as to look up the old police records. I found a jail photograph of this Harker person." He pulled open a desk drawer and removed a small piece of paper, passing it across. "This is a copy. As you know, I have friends down at the Hall."

Joshua picked up the print to study it. It was obviously made from an old tintype. "He doesn't look like a desperado. Except perhaps for the scar."

"I understand he claimed it was a dueling scar. More likely some lady tried to knife him."

"May I borrow this, Sir?"

"Why not? Now, are you ready to play cards, Your Highness?"

* * *

Mary Ellen read the headline on the late edition of the *Bulletin.* She glanced up to study Sophia's face, then down again to read the headline once more, this time out loud. *"Senator Shields Sued For Divorce. Friends Stunned, Marriage a Secret. Woman Claims They Were Wed 2 Years Ago."* Mary Ellen read on to herself, occasionally moving her lips or giving Sophia a strange look. "So you're going through with it," she said at last.

"Oh, yes. I have witnesses. I am suing for divorce on grounds of infidelity. I have a marriage contract, signed in secret by myself and by the Senator. Mr. Perry is certain it will stand up in court. The Senator won't get away with his shenanigans."

Mary Ellen put down the newspaper, neatly folded. "Perhaps this has something to do with that paper you mentioned—the blank one signed by Mr. Shields." Sophia merely smiled. In fact, she beamed at the other woman.

"Of course, I would not be a party to fraud," Mary Ellen said. "But since I know nothing about it, I guess I'm in the clear with Man and God. I will help you any way I can, as a friend."

"Thank you. I knew you would. This should be an interesting adventure. I shall be in court next week, for the preliminaries."

"And what will you do now?"

"Now? I believe I shall go and commiserate with my friend Marina."

Chapter 15

"**I** wanted to meet you," Heather said.

Simon sat stiffly in his chair. He looked like a man who was trying to relax but could not. Bannock had allowed Heather the use of his office for this meeting. "And I you." Simon smiled, looking like a man who tries to smile. "Does your mom know about this?"

"Hardly. She thinks I'm safely out of the way. I'm sure she would forbid me to meet with you, but I didn't allow her the chance. This is between the two of us. I was curious to inspect you—my mother must have found you attractive once. I wanted to see why. I have a great curiosity. I plan to be a journalist, you see." She gave him a beaming smile. He shifted in his chair.

"You brought me down here, across town, out of curiosity?"

"No. I wanted to offer you a business proposition. An opportunity, if you will."

"How old are you? Fourteen? Rather young to be in business."

She raised an eyebrow. "Do you want to hear? Yes? It's simply this: I will give you ten thousand dollars in scrip and bonds to go away and not trouble my mother again."

He blinked several times, then leaned forward across Bannock's desk. "Where would you get that kind of money?"

"I have influence. Are you interested or not?"

Simon drew the tip of his tongue across his lower lip. "When could I see the cash?"

"Right now. If you agree." She withdrew a package from her cloak, dropped it on the desk. "Are you agreed?"

"All right, if that's the way you feel about it. Unless, of course, Marina should determine to take me back into her home." He snatched up the brown paper parcel and tore it open. It was stuffed full of currency. He began counting, then halted after the first two or three bills. "What do you call this?"

Heather got up from her chair and drew herself to full height. "That, Sir, is official Imperial scrip issued by His Majesty, Emperor Norton the First, *dei gratia* Emperor of the United States and formerly Protector of Mexico. It is recognized as legal tender by a number of shops and restaurants in this city. The bonds are also issued by my friend the Emperor. They yield seven per cent interest on maturity."

Simon's face turned red. For a moment he looked as if about to explode. Then he burst into laughter. "I must say, young lady, you have a talent for persuasion. You would make a fine gambler or carnival act. Or perhaps a journalist. But I am afraid I must decline your kind offer." He picked up one bill and stuffed it into a pocket. "I believe I shall keep this one as a souvenir. "Good day to you." He turned and left the office. After a moment Bannock came in, a question in his eyes.

"Well, now I know what he's like," Heather said.

* * *

Joshua strolled to the end of the China Dock, stood gazing out across the bay for a few minutes, then turned and walked back. He noticed a German four masted barque in port. Men and equipment swarmed about her, loading and unloading at the same time. Joshua strolled through the crowd, wielding his manzanita walking stick like a scepter. He met Marina half way down the dock.

"I hope I'm not late?"

"Not at all, Madame. I am delighted to see you looking well." She gave the Emperor her arm, and they walked in silence toward the shore.

"You can guess why I wanted to see you," she said. "I am in need of your advice."

"Of course. Advice is one thing of which I have a

bountiful store. It's about this Simon Harker fellow?" She nodded, perhaps reluctant to speak his name. Joshua's boots made a hollow sound on the planks of the dock. Then they were walking up the cobbled street. "Have you made another appointment?"

"Not yet. I told him I would send him a note before the week is out. I can't wait too long, because Heather will be wanting to come home. And I mustn't impose on Ina much longer."

"Why not bring her home at once?"

"Oh, I couldn't. And take a chance on having Heather run into that awful man? There's no telling what effect he might have on her. I'm sure she would be upset."

"She might be stronger than you think." Marina shook her head.

"Do you recall when the Mayor finally called out the army, to protect the China Dock?" Joshua said. "When we were having the anti Chinese riots? The authorities did nothing, until the mob attacked the Dock. That was the last straw. The city stood to lose a great deal of money if the Dock were closed. That was the end of the riots."

"I know you were greatly concerned."

"In the end it's all about money, isn't it? Strange I took so long to see it. I think your Simon Harker is greatly impressed by cash."

"Would I had the army to help."

"I have a suggestion for you. Advice, if you will." Joshua explained his plan to her in a few words. She was puzzled and said so, but he urged her to ask no questions. In the end, she agreed. This afternoon she would send a note to Harker.

* * *

Next morning, Joshua strolled through grey drizzle, wishing for a real rain to wash away some of the gutter debris. He was not happy with the appearance of his streets; another proclamation might be called for, directed toward the Department of Street Cleaning. He neared the Chronicle building, noting the crowd gathered in front, and wandered closer to learn the news. *Senator Shields Denies Everything,* proclaimed the banner headline posted in the window. However, reading further, Joshua learned that he had not actually denied quite everything. He denied ever having signed a marriage contract, but he made no attempt to conceal the fact that Sophia had been his mistress. This promised to be the juiciest scandal the city had enjoyed in many a year.

Joshua's eye was caught by another paper posted to one side, with smaller headlines: *Marina Faces Bigamy Charge.* The story beneath was sketchy and less than accurate, but hinted at revelations to come. A woman nearby noticed him reading. "Well now, Your Grace!" She spoke with a broad Irish accent. "Quite a busy week, ain't it? Two such scandals at one time! Sometimes I wonder what will become of us all." Her toothless grin seemed to imply that whatever was to come, she was looking forward to it.

"I'm sure I couldn't say." He turned and moved off. He recalled that he'd promised Dr. Luk he would drop in for a check-up, and so turned in the direction of Chinatown. The drizzle had stopped falling, but the air was gray and damp.

Dr. Luk as usual, peered at Joshua's tongue, felt his pulses, poked and prodded. He made him lie down while he stuck needles in both shins. The needles had some strange herb attached to them, which the doctor proceeded to light and allow to burn. The air was filled with a pungent odor. When he was finished he said, "All is fine, I think. You are in good health, my Emperor. But you must not strain yourself. You may not dispel sadness with worry."

"Yes." Joshua rearranged his clothes. "You're right, I worry too much. I heard you are leaving us."

The doctor smiled. "News gets about. Yes, I am returning to Shanghai next month. San Francisco has been good to me, but not always easy. There are many in California who would be happy to see my people leave, except they need us for the mines and fields. I seek a more tranquil life, where I am welcome and where I have family."

"And I am sorry you must leave. I truly regret we have not been kinder to you."

"At least *you* have been. No charge for today's visit, my Emperor. Be kind to yourself."

* * *

The journal of Sophia Andrea Hull:

The first day in court was truly awful. I had expected mean looks from the Senator, but he would not even glance in my direction. It was all so cold. If only he had been a little kinder, I would not have embarked on this path in the first place. His lawyers will call handwriting experts to the stand, trying to prove the marriage contract a forgery. Mr. Perry assures me they can prove nothing of the sort, since the signatures are both genuine. One consolation is that I get to put on my best dresses in court; it's almost like being on stage. In fact, I have had an offer to take part in a production of The Merchant of Venice, despite my lack of acting experience. I'm told my notoriety will draw enormous crowds. I have not yet decided on my answer. I wonder how Marina is doing with that Harker person.

* * *

This time Marina met with Harker in Mr. Buxby's law office. When Harker came in, he kept glancing around and blinking in a nervous manner. He stopped and gaped when he saw Emperor Norton, occupying an oaken chair as if it were a throne, his beaver hat poised regally in the crook of one arm, his walking stick across his knees.

"Have you had occasion to meet our Emperor?" Marina asked.

Harker seemed to gather his wits. He straightened up,

then offered a low, sweeping bow. "An honor, Your Majesty, I must say. Your presence is most unexpected."

"Miss Marina desired to have a witness present at these negotiations," Joshua said.

As Harker took his seat, Marina shoved a newspaper across the table toward him. "Are you responsible for this notice?"

Harker glanced at the headlines, then assumed a wounded expression. "Certainly not, my dear. Did you really think I would stoop so low? I have no notion of how the papers got wind of our little disagreement."

"Don't 'my dear' me. Let's get to the point." She withdrew an envelope from her reticule. "This is some cash to carry you through the next week or so. I have considered your offer and have come to a tentative decision. I may be willing to take you back."

At this, Harker's eyes widened. He glanced back and forth between the two. He licked his lips, then stammered: "Why that's—wonderful, my dear. I must confess I am somewhat surprised, given your previous attitude. I'm—well, surprised."

"On one or two conditions."

His eyes narrowed again, wary. "Yes, what may they be?"

Marina looked up at the ceiling. "First of all, you must get rid of that awful beard. I wish to remember you as you once were. Also, I put enough money in that envelope for you to buy a decent readymade suit. Meet me here again in five days, on Saturday, when those two conditions are met. Then we shall discuss the matter further."

"Why, of course, my dear. I shall be delighted."

"And don't 'my dear' me."

* * *

Mary Ellen brought in the tea service herself, having given her maid the day off. Sophia thought the house seemed very quiet. She had been there nearly half an hour, and neither woman had spoken more than a few words. Finally Mary Ellen said, "Of course, I shall be learning of the day's proceedings in tomorrow's papers. The public does love a good scandal. But perhaps your own account may be more accurate, as well as timely."

Sophia took a deep breath. "It was quite humiliating. The Senator revealed the most intimate details of our life in open court. How we first met, how much money he paid me, and so on. He's really quite cruel. He doesn't hide the fact that his affair with this other woman has been going on for some time without my knowledge. In fact, there have been several others as well. He intimates I have been only one among many…" She began to weep, quietly.

Mary Ellen handed her a kerchief and poured her tea. After a few moments she said, "I am tempted to cast a hoodoo on this man. But that would be sinful. Does Mr. Perry think you have a chance of winning the case?"

"Oh, yes." She stifled her tears. "The handwriting experts can find no fault with the marriage contract. It's simply a matter of swaying the jury. And they're all men, after all."

"What story did you offer? I mean, about the contract. You must admit it's a bit odd."

Sophia sniffed and gave a little chuckle. "It's quite simple. Senator Shields told me what to write on the paper and we both signed it. We agreed to keep the marriage secret for two years because he was campaigning for reelection. Anyone familiar with David's character would find that quite believable. And the contract is binding, whether publicly registered or not. The alimony payments are practically mine."

Mary Ellen nodded. "I have heard something about your judge."

Sophia felt a twinge of anxiety at that. Mary Ellen's tone implied that she had heard something not good. "Yes?

What have you heard?"

"It's Judge Land, isn't it? From the Circuit Court? Did you know he was once a friend of Senator Bradley? Do you remember that tragedy?"

"Would I could forget. Mr. Perry killed him in a duel. It was quite fair and fully justified. But that was years ago. Are you telling me Bradley and Land were once close?"

"Bradley once saved Land's life back when they were both attorneys. A defeated opponent was hunting Land with a gun. Bradley pulled Land out of harm's way just in time. At least, that's how I heard the story. I don't know if Mr. Perry is aware of this."

Sophia shook her head. "No, perhaps not. At least he's not mentioned it to me. I must ask him when I see him this evening."

"You are seeing Mr. Perry tonight?"

"Yes." She smiled. "I know you won't mention it to a soul—we have become quite intimate, you see."

"Ah, yes," Mary Ellen said. "I see."

* * *

For once, Sophia was early for Court. She lingered in the corridor, enjoying attention from reporters and curious spectators. She made it a point to dress in a different outfit each day; today she wore a dove gray silk with mother-of-pearl buttons. Her hat was equally conservative, with a single ostrich feather.

"Where is Mr. Perry today?" the *Chronicle* reporter asked. She gave him a winning smile.

"He is called momentarily away on other business, about his ranch, but he expects to return tomorrow. His assistant, Mr. Paynter, will be more than adequate for the job today. I believe we are due to be subjected to more testimony from the handwriting experts." Before she had to answer another question, a bell rang and people began filing into the courtroom. She waited till the others had gone in, so as to make a more dramatic entrance.

True to expectations, there was more to be heard from the experts; there was one called by the defense, and one by the claimant. They seemed to agree with each other on some points, and to be at each others' throats on others. There were microscopes, lenses and charts occupying most of the exhibit table. This being a hot day, all the windows and doors were left open. After an hour or so, Sophia found it hard to stay awake. She was startled when she noticed people getting up to file past the exhibits. She nudged her attorney.

"I wasn't listening. What is happening?"

"Nothing to worry about. They're looking at your letters under microscopes. I mean the *Dear Wife* letters."

"Oh, those." The Senator had been indiscreet enough to send her several notes in the past, addressing her as "Dear Wife." She had of course introduced these as evidence. She had also taken the trouble to add "Dear Wife" to a few other letters which had not been so addressed. "What is it they hope to discover?"

"Whether *Dear Wife* was added before or after the ink was dry on the rest of the paper. They claim they're able to tell by the way the ink cracks when the paper is folded." He gave her a reassuring smile.

"How deadly dull. Still, I suppose I may as well look." She got up and made her way to the table. The Senator was not in court today; there were rumors he wasn't feeling well. More likely, she thought, he was simply bored. He had a team of four attorneys manning his battlements. She took her turn at the microscopes, peering at hugely magnified letters embedded with fractures and wrinkles in the long-dried ink. "How dreadful," she thought.

Then there was the lunch recess. Probably the afternoon session would have been equally dull, except that one of the Senator's lawyers unexpectedly called another witness to the stand. Sophia recognized one of the maids from the hotel where the Senator had previously installed her. She listened, half interested, until she realized the maid was actually lying.

"...so I heard her say she forged all those letters and the contract, so she did..."

Sophia got to her feet, furious not at the maid, but at the lawyer who had obviously paid her to say these things. "You ought to be horsewhipped! Bringing a woman here to say such things about me! I will see you flogged, Sir! In fact, I will shoot you myself!"

The hearing room went into uproar. The judge's gavel banged. He ordered Mr. Paynter to restrain her. The latter did his best, without much effect.

"Sit down or I'll suspend these proceedings!" the judge roared.

"How much did you pay her?" Sophia demanded. The maid, still on the stand, looked about to faint. The defense lawyer had turned beet red. "I swear I will shoot you!" Sophia ignored Mr. Paynter's tugs at her sleeve. She opened her reticule and took out the double derringer she usually carried. She pointed it at the attorney, whose face went from red to chalk white. Then, perhaps realizing where she was, she dropped the pistol to the desk. She sat down and surveyed the crowded room; some of the spectators were standing, others trying to make themselves smaller. "You may proceed, your honor. I will say no more."

Judge Land took a deep breath. "Bailiff, please impound the lady's pistol."

That about ended the day's business. The defense lawyer said he would resume the next day. The judge ordered Sophia to be searched next time she showed up, and called a recess. Mr. Paynter mopped sweat from his brow.

"That was wonderful," someone said behind her as she left the hearing room. She turned to discover Heather, cradling a thick notebook.

"What was?" Sophia felt confused, wondering herself what had just happened. She had not realized she was so angry.

"Your performance with the gun," Heather said. "It was great theater. It's bound to impress the public and the court. A Wronged Woman's Outrage. That's the headline I'm giving Mr. Bannock for tomorrow's edition."

"Oh. Yes. You're one of those reporters, aren't you?" Sophia looked at the ceiling a moment. "I think you're right. A Wronged Woman's Outrage. That's not bad. In fact, it's quite good. Yes, I like that. See you in court, Heather." She turned away, then halted. "How is that problem coming with your mother's unwelcome visitor?"

Heather grinned. "Quite a scandal, actually. Although none of the papers have their facts right. But it's enough to bring folks in droves to the theater, hoping to catch a glimpse of Mom. And here, she thought it would keep them away! We're making piles of money."

Sophia shook her head. "San Francisco gets stranger all the time."

* * *

On Saturday, Joshua enjoyed tea in Marina's parlor. She showed him Heather's latest report in the *Bulletin*. Joshua shook his head slowly, not quite knowing what to make of that business.

"One good thing, for me at least," Marina said, "Sophia's divorce scandal has diverted attention from my own problems. There hasn't been a word in any of the papers all week."

"Truly a blessing. Although, I'm told the publicity has not harmed your theater attendance."

"No, but I could do without it." She was silent a moment, giving him a thoughtful look. "Not that we can't use the extra trade. I wasn't going to trouble you with my other worries, but the fact is business has not been good. What with the financial panic and all, attendance has been down and creditors are calling in their loans. The theater is heavily in debt, and we are in peril of foreclosure. So you see, I am not as wealthy as Mr. Harker seems to think."

"Heather told me you were making a lot of money."

"It would appear so, from the recent receipts, but it's not enough to make up for the debt. Please don't mention this to Heather, I wouldn't cause her worry."

"I shall not, of course." He glanced at the grandfather clock in the corner. Its slow ticking was the only sound in this room. "When do you expect Mr. Harker?"

"Momentarily. I wish you would explain your plan before he arrives."

Joshua might have done so, but as he opened his mouth the doorbell rang. The maid admitted Simon Harker. Neither Joshua nor Marina rose, but he took a seat on the couch without waiting for invitation.

"My dear. It's so nice to see you looking well."

"I am not your dear. I see you have cleaned yourself up a bit."

Harker stood and turned slowly, arms held out. "Do you like the suit? I even went to the bath house last night, though it wasn't Saturday yet. Stylish, don't you think?"

"Yes, and you have shaved as I asked. Definitely an improvement."

Without invitation, Harker took a seat on the other side of the room in the shade, away from the windows. "This heat is unusual for Frisco, ain't it?"

"My dear Sir." Joshua rose to his feet and took a step in Harker's direction. He stopped, leaning on his walking stick. "It would seem you are unfamiliar with my Imperial Proclamation of 1872. I must credit you with ignorance, and so forego the legal fine on this occasion. The Proclamation reads, and I quote: *Whoever after due and proper warning shall be heard to utter the abominable word 'Frisco,' which has no linguistic or other warrant, shall be deemed guilty of a High Misdemeanor, and shall pay into the Imperial Treasury as penalty the sum of twenty-five dollars.*

"You may consider this due and proper warning, and so be advised."

Harker's eyes widened, glancing from Joshua to Marina and back again. "Yes Sir, if you say so."

Joshua half turned back to his seat, then stopped. "Have either of you heard The Tale of the Talking Jackrabbit? No? I heard it from a miner just returned from Hangtown, so I know it to be true. It seems there was a young fellow by the name of Blount, a nice enough fellow, but given to talking a great deal. Allow him into any room and he would soon bore everyone to tears. Well, Sir, one evening he was killing time at the Hangtown Saloon, bending the ears of anyone who would listen. Eventually, the evening growing late, he decided to leave and make his way home, which was the diggings where he was employed at scratching up clay, somewhere up river."

At mention of the Name Blount, Harker gave a start and his face paled, but Joshua seemed not to notice. He continued:

"He began to make his way along the trail by moonlight. But he hadn't gone far, when a voice called out, 'Blount! You talk too damn much!' The fellow looked around and could see no one. Finally, he spotted a jackrabbit sitting on a stump. He demanded to know if the creature had addressed him. 'Yes,' it said. 'I said you talk too damn much.' Well, Mr. Blount became quite excited at this, never before having encountered a verbose bunny. He turned around and ran as fast as he could back to the Hangtown Saloon. Once there, he loudly proclaimed he had discovered a talking jackrabbit, and urged everyone there to come outside so he could show them.

The whole crowd came out, and followed the poor fellow up the trail. There, sure enough, was a jackrabbit sitting unconcerned on a redwood stump. But despite young Blount's repeated urging, the critter refused to utter a word. Blount about worked himself into a frenzy, dancing round the stump, pleading and shouting at the poor rabbit, trying to get him to say something. But not a word was uttered. Finally, Blount's drinking companions got fed up with the whole thing. They beat up the young man, blackened an eye, bloodied his nose, tore off his clothes, threw him in the ditch, and went back to the saloon.

Then, when they were all gone and it was quiet once again, the jackrabbit regarded Blount with a baleful eye, and said, 'See what I mean, Blount? You talk too damn much.'"

Joshua stopped and regarded Harker in silence for a moment.

"What's the point of that tale?" Harker asked.

Joshua shrugged. "I suppose it's just that one should be willing to listen to advice when it's offered." He took another step closer. "Now, perhaps you will accept a word of advice from myself, your Emperor."

"And what advice would that be, pray tell?"

"To look for a better quality line of theatrical supplies."

"What are you talking about, Old Man?"

Joshua glanced at Marina. "Miss Marina here has considerable experience in the theatrical world. I refer to such things as costume and makeup. What do you think, Marina? Is it a good job?"

"Is what a good job?"

"Ah. Perhaps you cannot see well in the shadows here. Please come a bit closer."

Marina, looking puzzled, arose and approached Harker, who seemed to shrink back. She studied his face.

"Notice anything amiss?"

She shook her head. "I'm not sure. There's something not quite right."

"Allow me to refresh your memory." Joshua withdrew from his jacket a brown envelope from which he extracted a photograph. "Remember your husband's scar?"

"Of course." She glanced at the picture. "Oh, yes, I see."

Joshua handed it to Harker. "I must say you did a fairly good job working from memory alone, as you must have. But as you can see, the dueling scar on your cheek is slightly off. The one in the picture is closer to the neck, and a bit shorter."

"I can explain that—"

"I'm sure you can. But I must say, it's not a good quality job. The spirit gum is melting in the heat." Without warning, he reached over, yanked off the scar on Harker's jaw, and handed it to Marina. "What do you think, Madame? Is this good quality or not?

Marina was staring, white faced, at Harker. "It's not him. That's not my husband."

"No." Joshua withdrew another piece of paper from the brown envelope. "Mr. Bannock was able to obtain a report—"

"*That's not him!* There's a resemblance, but it isn't Simon. I thought, of course he would have changed after all these years, but now I see it's not him at all! He's fooled me! *What have you done with Simon? Have you murdered him?*"

Joshua touched her arm to restrain her. "Let us not make wild accusations. This man is guilty of fraud and blackmail, but not murder. This is a report from Mexico, by way of the Los Angeles Sheriff. It arrived only yesterday, so I've not had time to discuss it with you. This man's name is Ira Blount. He and Harker were cell mates for about a year, in Tijuana. Harker died of syphilis while in jail. Blount here, must have got his entire history. He decided to capitalize on it. He nearly succeeded, or so he thinks."

Blount had risen to his feet. "I could still make a lot of trouble for you—"

Joshua's walking stick rose and fell to the floor with a

thunderous boom. "And you could go to prison for extortion! Or worse. The San Francisco Committee of Vigilance was never officially disbanded, and I am still a member." His stick struck the floor again. "You Sir, shall depart this house in the next ten seconds! And you shall leave this city within 24 hours! Or you may find yourself dangling at the end of a rope!" Another boom from the stick.

Blount backed away. He opened his mouth to say something, but stopped as Joshua took a step closer. Then he was out the front door and gone.

Marina sat down and slowly poured two cups of tea. "Well, that's done with."

"And I must say it was rather fun, wasn't it?" He laughed. They both laughed. And laughed, and laughed.

Chapter 16

The next three weeks were no fun for Sophia. In fact, they were an ordeal. Both sides having presented evidence and arguments, the jury ruled in favor of Sophia. She celebrated by throwing a party, at Perry's home. But then the Senator's attorneys filed an appeal the next day. The headline in the *Bulletin* said: **Senator Shields Vows She Will Never Get a Dime.** Sophia's mood plummeted. Perry told her they would have to start all over again. She went to see Mary Ellen.

"Do you wish me to read the cards once more?"

Sophia gave a shrug. "If you wish, but that's not why I came. I just wanted to talk. What do you think of my chances?"

Mary Ellen looked long into her eyes. "You are a strong woman. But the Senator is a powerful man. I don't know who is the strongest, but I know something you perhaps have not thought of. That is, that the lawyers are stronger than both of you. The Senator exists only at the sufferance of his attorneys. The same is true of yourself. It is the Law that rules both your lives."

Sophia chewed at her lip. It was a nervous habit she had lately developed. "I'm not sure what you mean. I'll have to think it over. What most upset me in court today was that they are still claiming the Senator and I were not married, that my contract is not legal. They even go so far as to say it's a complete forgery!"

"Which, in fact, it is."

Sophia started. "Whoever told you that? It's not true. The Senator told me what to write, and we both signed it. So it's a legal contract." She broke off at Mary Ellen's continued stare. "At least, that's what I remember." She passed a hand across her eyes. "Sometimes I have trouble remembering things."

Mary Ellen arose. "Let me fetch some fresh tea."

* * *

Then, two weeks after that conversation, Heather came home in the afternoon with some shocking news.

"The Senator died!" she announced.

Marina was in a rocker, where she'd been reading a romance novel. She put the book down slowly. "You mean Senator Shields? What on earth do you mean, he died?"

Heather fell onto the sofa. She spread her hands as if helpless. "Dead. I just came from court. They announced it today. Heart failure, I guess. Then his lawyers went on with the trial as if nothing had happened."

"How horrible. And Sophia was in court? How did she take it?"

"I can't say. Had no chance to speak to her. She never said a word or changed expression; just stared at the lawyers. At the end of the day they rushed her out through the mob."

"She must be in shock." Marina stood and paced the floor. "I shall send her a note of commiseration. No, that might not be appropriate. Perhaps I should go and see her. The trial goes on as usual, you say?"

"Well, of course. There's the Senator's estate to be settled. He had millions, you know. This might make it even harder for Sophia."

"Yes, I can well imagine. It's all quite confusing, isn't it? I believe I really ought to visit her. I know, I'll bring the Emperor. Perhaps he can find a way to cheer her."

* * *

Sophia felt cheerful. At first she thought she ought to feel sad about the Senator's death, but then she discovered she didn't. Today she was cheerful about the fact that she was not sad. It was Sunday, and court in recess. Mr. Perry's butler admitted her visitors.

"I'm so happy to see you both!" she beamed at them, when they were seated in the parlor. While Mr. Perry's house was not quite wealthy, the room was well furnished with over-stuffed, dusty furniture and lots of knick knacks.

"You're looking well," Marina said. "I had thought you might be in seclusion."

Sophia had been trying on one of her best ball gowns. She did a little pirouette in the middle of the room. "As to that, wearing black would not become me, I think. I suppose I should mourn, but I don't feel like a widow. In fact, I won't be one for long. But how does the world find you today, Your Majesty?" Turning toward Joshua.

Joshua stroked his beard in thought. "It finds me well. I was sorry to hear of your loss, but perhaps it was not so much a loss as we presumed?"

Sophia gave a short giggle. "I hope I don't sound calloused, but the fact is, the Senator and I had not been close for some time. And then he chose to abuse me so! It's so hard for a lady to manage on her own, especially after being rejected by her own husband! Please do not judge me harshly. I must be honest in saying I feel mainly a sense of relief. And I may have some wonderful news in the near future, but I'm not to speak of that just yet."

"Well." Marina got to her feet and Joshua followed. "I must say I'm happy to hear you are well, Sophia. Although these must be trying times for you. Joshua and I could only stop by for a moment, so we'll be on our way."

"You won't be staying for tea? Ah well, if you must. I do hope you will both come to the soirée we are planning."

"A soirée? May I ask what is the occasion?"

"Oh. I spoke too soon, didn't I? I promised Mr. Perry I wouldn't breathe a word about it just yet. But then—since you are both such intimate friends… if you swear to say nothing?" She paused, looking from Joshua to Marina and back.

"If you wish. I can see you're terribly excited about something. Mum's the word, Sophia."

Sophia glanced around, as if searching for

eavesdroppers. She took a step closer and spoke in a voice above a whisper.

"Mr. Perry has proposed marriage. And I have accepted."

* * *

Three weeks later, the soirée took place as promised. Since Mr Perry's home was too small for all the invited guests, he rented the dining room at the Lick House. The cream of San Francisco Society showed up. Sophia had sufficient notoriety, if not respectability, to attract the best the city had to offer. A liveried butler thumped his cane and introduced each guest as they entered. Miss Marina came early, accompanied by her daughter. Later on, Joshua made his entrance in his best uniform, duly presented as "Joshua Norton I, dei gratia Emperor of the United States."

Mary Ellen, as well, appeared; her ball gown outshone even Sophia's. Sophia was well aware that Mr. Perry did not approve of this person, but she had insisted on the invitation. Some of the city's *nouveau riche* also disapproved of a woman of color in society, but most of the older residents took the matter in stride. Sophia hardly left her side for most of the evening.

"I see," Mary Ellen said, "that Mr. Perry combines business with pleasure." She nodded in his direction across the room, where he was engrossed in conversation with two of his attorneys.

"Yes, he's terribly serious about this legal case of mine. He's highly optimistic. Did you hear Judge Land has been elevated to the State Supreme Court? He's the one who ruled in our favor, you know. Or at least the jury did, and he accepted their decision. So he'll be sitting on my case a second time."

"I hope you won't be disappointed, dear. Judges have been known to change their minds."

"He wouldn't dare," Sophia said. She stared across the

room at Perry. "Not if he knows what's good for him."

About midnight, Perry mounted the stage to announce the betrothal of himself and Mrs. Sophia Shields. By that time, Marina had gone home with her daughter.

* * *

Marina next day read the *Bulletin* with a glum expression. She found a review of Sophia's party on the second page, together with another update on her legal problems, but that was not what made Marina glum. It was the financial reports.

"Another bank failure," she read aloud. "I don't like the news of late."

Heather had been busy writing something at her desk. "Aren't we making a profit still? I mean at the theater?"

Marina smiled. "You're still a child, Heather. You don't understand high finance. We can make a profit and still go broke. I have been able to hold off the bank, but the mortgage is about to fall due. They won't be put off any longer."

Heather stared into space. "Could we be put out of house and home?"

Marina took a moment to answer. "I shall not lie to you. Yes, it's quite possible."

"Perhaps Emperor Norton could issue a proclamation."

"A lot of good his proclamations have done himself. Then again, perhaps he has the right idea. He owns nothing and has nothing to lose. If he needs money, he just prints it. Who is to say he's wrong?"

"Most folks say he's mad."

"After reading the news, I wonder who is maddest," Marina said.

Heather came across the room to look at the newspaper. "Do you think Sophia will be happy in her marriage?"

"Dear, I hope so."

* * *

The Journal of Sophia Andrea Hull:

My goodness, Mr. Perry does have energy. He has been busy in court all week. There was hardly time for the wedding. But I have never felt happier. He is a good husband, and has more than enough energy left for the bedroom. We are quite optimistic about my claim for back alimony and a share of the Senator's estate. Next week Mr. Perry will go to Sacramento to present my case before the Supreme Court. That should settle the matter once and for all.

Sophia did not go to Sacramento, since there was no need for her to give testimony; the arguments were all about legal precedents and discovery of evidence and such, which Sophia barely understood. Mr. Perry was gone three days. In the meantime, she spent some hours at Mary Ellen's home.

"When did you first discover you could hear the spirits?" Mary Ellen asked.

Sophia pulled at the corners of a purple silk kerchief, twisting and turning it. "I'm not sure just when, but it has been quite recent. They tell me all sorts of interesting things, though I'm not sure they hear me when I speak to them."

"What sort of things do they tell you?"

Sophia smiled and held the kerchief to her ear. She shut her eyes a moment, listening. "They tell me what other folks are doing. They inform me that at this moment Mr. Perry is preparing a brief in an anteroom. A secretary is helping him."

Mary Ellen sipped at her tea. "My dear, I must tell you. Listening to spirits is not always safe or wise. Perhaps you might do better to put up the kerchief and not listen for a time. Listen instead to those around you."

Sophia chuckled. "Oh, but I can do both, can't I? And

it's not as if these are *evil* spirits. In fact, they're quite friendly and nice."

"And do they speak to you of other people besides Mr. Perry?"

Sophia shut her eyes again. "Sometimes. Oh. Yes, I see. It appears the Emperor has just arrived at Miss Marina's home. They're having quite a serious discussion, it seems. But I can't hear what it's about."

Chapter 17

"**A** sad day," Joshua said. "So you say the theater will close at the end of the month. Truly a sad day."

"Yes." Marina's eyes were red from weeping. "I suppose I shall lose the house as well. They're saying it's all because of the greed of the railroad. I wouldn't know about that. It's just hard times is all."

"Boom and bust," Joshua said. "I came here to California during the rush, when it was all boom. Then I myself went bust. But that was before I became Emperor. I must confess I am for once at a loss what to do."

"You have helped us all with your gentleness. You need do no more."

Joshua studied the grain of his walking stick, or scepter. He said, "There is perhaps one thing. You know my attorney friend, Mr. Buxby. He may have some advice."

"I doubt it. But if you think I should speak to him…"

"No, there's no need. I will see him myself. However—have you told your daughter the unhappy news?"

"Yes, I can hardly deceive her. She knows all about it. She thinks we should go off on a world tour."

"Perhaps so. Well, then. Please ask Heather to meet me at Mr. Buxby's office tomorrow afternoon. Say, 1 p.m. He always sees me without an appointment, I'm sure there will be no problem."

"But why Heather…?"

Joshua shrugged. "She can bear a message if there is one. There's no need for you to make the trip downtown."

Marina gave him a puzzled look. "I suppose she can do no harm. I'll tell her directly."

* * *

Judge Perry arrived on the boat from Sacramento the next afternoon, at about the same time Joshua and Heather went to Mr. Buxby's office. He and Sophia had a long, heated discussion. Later, Sophia wrote in her journal.

> *Dear Diary,*
>
> *Mr. Perry is furious. It seems his trip to court was a fiasco. Judge Land reversed his own previous decision and declared my marriage to Senator Shields was not legal. I don't understand the twisting of his legal reasoning—now he declares the document a forgery, and even if it wasn't it's still not legal because of not being registered. What a farce. Mr. Perry lost his temper and berated the judge. Now Mr. Perry is cited for contempt and must appear in court next week to answer the charge. He is beside himself. He says he will personally horsewhip Judge Land. Unfortunately, he did make the error of saying this in the courtroom. I believe I shall go to the garden and hear what the spirits have to say.*

* * *

Buxby was occupied with a client when Joshua arrived, but his secretary asked him to wait. Joshua busied himself with the front page of the *Bulletin,* until Heather came in about ten minutes later.

"It is so unlike you to be tardy," Joshua said, rising.

"The street car broke down. I had to walk."

"I'm sorry. But don't concern yourself; Mr. Buxby is engaged at the moment."

"What's this all about, Joshua?"

Joshua combed his beard with his fingers. "You sound suspicious, my lady."

"You're up to something, I can tell. What have you got up your sleeve, Mr. Emperor?"

"Nothing at all." He pulled back his cuffs to demonstrate. "Merely this tin box, which is in plain sight, not up my sleeve."

"You're not fooling me, Joshua. You can pull the wool

over Mother's eyes, but—" She broke off as Buxby's office door opened and a man with a bowler hat in one hand and a briefcase in the other charged out. Buxby put his face out a moment later.

"Yet another unsatisfied customer," he grinned. Then his face turned somber and he said in a lower tone, "Railroad attorney. But I won't burden you with the details. Come in, both of you. To what do I owe this auspicious visit?"

Joshua waited until he and Heather were seated across from Buxby at his desk. He glanced around at the shut door and lowered his voice. "A small bit of legal business, Sir. If you won't mind."

"Not at all. Tell me, please." Buxby folded his hands before him. Heather was staring at Joshua. Joshua cleared his throat.

"I felt it best, under the circumstances, to have a lawful witness present during a minor transaction. In case there should be questions in the future."

Buxby glanced at each of them, wearing his professional-serious face. "And what sort of transaction might this be? Some sort of contract?"

"No, Sir. More in the nature of transfer of property." Joshua turned to face Heather. "As you are aware, dear Heather, your mother is in some financial difficulty."

"She told me."

"Ah. Yes. Well, I have given the problem some thought. You see, I have grown lately to feel some disappointment in my own position. I had thought the nation would welcome and honor me as their rightful Emperor. To some extent they have, at least in this city. I am grateful for the privilege of serving as beneficent dictator. However, I have lately grown to accept the knowledge that my dreams of dwelling in a palace on a golden throne are not to be." Here he glanced at Buxby, whose expression had not changed.

"Likewise, I had hoped to have a golden crown one

day, studded with jewels. But this item also is withheld. Perhaps it's just as well—I think the beaver hat suits me better." He smiled. Buxby and Heather said nothing, waiting for him to continue.

"Therefore, I have come to the conclusion there is no use in my holding on to the crown jewels any longer. I therefore present them to you." He held out the tin box for Heather to take. After a moment she reached for it and gingerly opened the lid. She looked up at him again.

"Are they real?"

"Oh, yes, quite. From South Africa, you see. Perhaps Mr. Buxby would care to examine them." Heather passed the box to Buxby, who withdrew a lens from his desk drawer. He picked up several diamonds one after another, peering closely. Heather and Joshua could see his greatly enlarged eye blinking rapidly.

"Yes, they are genuine. I can tell by their cut and refraction." He took out one gem and turned to the window. With great care, he scratched a letter N on the glass. Then he returned the gems to Heather.

"You are presenting her with the entire box, Sir?"

"Yes. Any one gem sold at auction should bring enough to pay off the theater mortgage. As to the others, Miss Heather, you are free to do with them as you wish. Keep them for a dowry, or travel around the earth and never marry. As you will, do what you must."

Heather screwed up her face. "Why not give them to my mother?"

Joshua glanced at Buxby. "Because she has no need of more than one. She has made her own way, and will continue. You have the future before you, and no one may tell what portends. You will live to see this new century coming, with unknown miracles and dangers. Wealth will help you through. I don't know what you may choose, Miss Heather, but a few riches may make your choices easier. Mr. Buxby, would you be so good as to make out a receipt?"

"What will you do?" Heather asked.

Joshua grinned and gave his stick a thump on the floor. "Enjoy life. This evening I shall attend a lecture at the Academy of Sciences. It will be about the theories of Mr. Darwin. It should be great fun."

* * *

The sky came down as mist, changing to soft rain. Joshua did not mind the rain. He had his umbrella, but made no move to open it. California Street grew quiet this time of evening, most of the businesses closed and the shopkeepers had gone home to dinner. It came to him that he had no more need of Dr. Luk. His sadness had gone. He sensed a warm uprising in his breast that must be happiness.

Although he had not thought about his crown jewels often, he realized they must have been worrying at some part of his soul all this time. It was a relief to be rid of them. Now he was entirely free. At last, he was really like those two mangy curs, Lazarus and Bummer; owning nothing, but free to dine where they pleased. Perhaps, he thought, after the lecture I shall eat in Chinatown again. Restaurants stay open late there.

He was looking forward to the lecture. The Academy of Sciences attracted thoughtful folks. He might find someone to enter into discussion afterward, or perhaps a small group. With luck, he might be invited to dinner.

He felt delight in the world. Despite the evening drizzle, colors appeared brighter, the air electric. Approaching the corner of California and DuPont, he glanced up at St. Mary's Cathedral. He had never before paid much attention to the building. Constructed entirely of red brick, he had always thought it rather ugly. Tonight it seemed to glow with an inner light, and he found a strange beauty in it. He read the peculiar motto inscribed in large letters on its steeple:

Son, observe the time and fly from evil.

Yes, he decided. *The time grows late. That is what I shall do. I shall fly from evil.* He felt that he was flying, as his body sank slowly to the pavement.

A young policeman was nearby. He rushed to the Emperor's side to cradle his head, while blowing his whistle at a passing carriage. He bawled orders at the driver to get the Emperor to the hospital. But by that time, Joshua Norton had already found his golden crown.

Chapter 18

The Journal of Sophia Andrea Hull:

Dear me. These are difficult times. Mr. Perry and I, William I mean, have been spending three days at his country house. It has been quiet here, but so, so hot. William said he wanted to cool off before his next appearance in court, but it hasn't quite worked out that way. He is still furious with Judge Land. He vows revenge if ever he catches him outside the court room.

A copy of the San Francisco Call was delivered this morning. I was shocked to discover that Emperor Norton has passed away. It seems he was walking in North Beach on his way to a lecture, when he fell in the street. How sad. I'm afraid the poor man was quite mad, after all. How could I ever have suspected he was hoarding a secret treasure? They say his room was searched, but nothing of value was found. The funeral was yesterday—the paper says there were ten thousand people attending. The procession was two miles long. I'm sorry I missed it, it must have been a spectacle.

On Monday William and I must travel back to Sacramento to face his charge of contempt. We shall be taking the afternoon train. William doesn't know yet about my ability to hear the spirits. I will explain when the time is ripe. For now, I shall wait till he's not around, while I consult them about our best course of action. I remain hopeful regarding my appeal.

* * *

From the San Francisco *Evening Bulletin:*

JUDGE LAND HIRES BODYGUARD
EXCLUSIVE TO THE BULLETIN

MORE DEVELOPMENTS IN
SENSATIONAL DIVORCE TRIAL

The *Bulletin* has learned through confidential sources that Judge Land, who last week cited Sophia Hull's attorney for contempt, has appointed a personal bodyguard. It is said he fears for his life due to recent death threats against him on the part of her attorney. Said attorney is Mr. William Perry. Astute readers may recall that Mr. Perry was once notorious for having slain our beloved Senator Bradley in a duel. Judge Land's bodyguard is said to have been appointed from the ranks of United States marshals...

* * *

The railroad engine is black, smooth, and shiny as jet. Black smoke billows from its funnel, and the sound of its pistons as it approaches the station are like black boots stamping on the ground.

Sophia writes for the last time in her journal:

I sense that something—I know not what—is about to happen. That it will be something unpleasant, I am certain. We have been all night on this train. I slept most comfortably in dear William's arms. But the spirits have been trying to warn me. I hear their voices as shrieks without words. Early this morning we learned from another passenger that by coincidence Judge Land is aboard. At this discovery, William's rage only seemed to increase. We are approaching the station, where passengers may alight and break fast in the railroad restaurant. I pleaded with William not to go, but he insists he has nothing to fear from the judge or his bodyguard. He hopes he may encounter the man so the judge may be humiliated in public. I have misgivings. I shall remain with William come what may. I offered to bring my pistol, but he ordered me to leave it on the train.

The engine slows, screeches, hisses, squeals, comes at last to a stop. The conductor emerges, placing a step-stool before each of the car doors. There are three passenger cars, as well as the baggage car and diner. One by one, passengers climb down, stretch themselves, look around with bleary eyes, head for the restaurant door. One of the passengers is Judge Land of the State Supreme Court. He marches straight ahead, looking neither to right nor left. By his side is a short fellow wearing a cheap gray suit. Unlike the judge, he scans his path at every moment, eyes never at rest. He himself is nondescript, unnoticed, yet he misses nothing.

The judge and the man with him enter the restaurant where a dozen or so other passengers are already seated at long tables. Judge Land takes his place with the rest, expecting no special treatment. The restaurant is known for fast service, vital for a railroad establishment. The two men give their orders and are served almost at once. The judge begins to eat. So does his companion, but his eyes are always busy.

A few minutes later, William Perry and Sophia enter arm in arm. They appear to be a loving couple. Few give them a second glance. But Perry's head jerks as he spots the judge. He releases Sophia's arm and strides forward.

What happens then takes but a few seconds. Perry crosses the room; the judge has not looked up and does not see him. His companion, a United States marshal, puts down his fork and starts to rise. Before he can get on his feet, Perry reaches the judge. The judge looks up at him, startled.

William Perry raises his right hand and slaps the judge hard across the cheek, once, twice. Some food particles spurt from the judge's mouth onto his beard.

By this time—only a few seconds have passed—the marshal has regained his feet. He reaches inside his coat, withdraws a pistol, and fires directly into Perry's chest.

* * *

Sometime later, Marina announced a memorial concert in memory of Emperor Norton. Proceeds would go toward construction of a new hospital. Before the concert, Mary Ellen came backstage to pay her respects. Marina, in her dressing room, gave her a warm embrace.

"I'm so happy you could come. I know how much Joshua admired you."

"And I him. There are so many familiar faces here, enemies and friends alike. The Emperor is here in spirit."

"Indeed. I'm sorry Sophia couldn't be here. I heard what you did for her. I imagine it was the only right thing."

Mary Ellen sighed. "I fear it was. She never got over Mr. Perry's death. And she could find no other attorneys to help with her lawsuit, you know. She could have remained in the country, but she *would* come back to San Francisco. She took to wandering the streets. She was quite sad at the end; hotels all refused her. I thought of giving her shelter myself, but to tell the truth I feared she might burn the house down. She was quite unhappy."

"So you had her committed to the asylum. Do you suppose she will ever leave that place?"

"Who can say? Not even I can predict the future."

The concert that night became the talk of the town. There was a string quartet playing Mozart, as well as singers from the opera. In recent years Marina had rarely performed herself, but tonight she chose to close out the show. She sang her old songs and played her old fiddle, and did four encores. Heather, in the front row, took notes for the *Bulletin*.

A month later, Marina and Heather took the boat to Stockton, to visit Sophia at the State Insane Asylum.

"Such a delightful young lady!" Sophia beamed when she caught sight of Heather. "I'll wager you have dozens of suitors for your hand."

Heather gave her a serious look. "I intend to be a journalist. I doubt I'll have time to marry, though I may take a lover. Soon I shall travel around the world."

Marina laughed nervously. "Heather is precocious and creative. Much like her father; she does as she wills."

"I myself have been married twice," Sophia said. "Perhaps she has the right idea."

Marina wanted to change the subject. "You're wearing a lovely dress, Sophia."

"Thank you. I always felt green best becomes me. Have you walked about the grounds yet? The garden is lovely this time of year." They began to stroll. A few other inmates wandered about, a few of them carrying on conversations with themselves. "I have quite forgiven Mary Ellen for having me sent here. Please tell her so. It's quite pleasant. We have no end of amusements, and people are so generous. Of course, everyone has read about me in the papers..." She trailed off.

"I understand there will be a celebration at Christmas."

"Oh yes. There are frequent shows and parties, all in my honor of course. And if I can find no one else to converse with, I always have my spirits." She pulled a silk handkerchief from her sleeve.

"Well, then. I'm so glad you're well. But I see it's nearly time for my performance."

Marina had volunteered to perform for the inmates and staff. She had brought no other performers with her, but she had her fiddle. Everyone assembled in the common room, and she mounted the little stage. One of the inmates, as introduction, played *Beautiful Dreamer* on an upright piano. Then Marina stepped forward and began to sing. Her listeners leaned forward in their seats with rapt attention. Marina felt she was back in the old Missouri music hall. She sang with all her heart, for Sophia, for Joshua Norton, and for Randall most of all. She sang and played her fiddle for an hour and a half, until all but exhausted. At last, as a final song, she sang her old favorite. Some of the audience joined in:

Let us pause in life's pleasures and count its many tears,
While we all sup sorrow with the poor…
Many days you have lingered around my cabin door;

Oh hard times, hard times come again no more.

They were the finest audience she had ever known.

The End

About the author:

The author was born a long time ago. He spent three years in the US Army where he learned a lot of vital skills, such as how to use a soldering iron and screwdriver, as well as how to make the bed, mop the floor, and wash dishes. He grew up and spent most of his life in San Francisco. After obtaining a useless liberal arts degree, he became a social worker and did more than 20 years in the mean streets of New York City, San Francisco, and rural California. He is now devoted to writing books, which he should have been doing in the first place. He has written some science fiction and fantasy, but is now mainly interested in tales of the Old West. Some previous publications:

- THE TERRORIST PLOT AT GOPHERVILLE, © 2006, Lulu.com

- GOLD, A TALE OF THE CALIFORNIA GOLD RUSH, © 2008, ePress Online

- JOURNEY TO RHYOLITE, © 2009, Norlights Press

- CHAPEL PERILOUS, © 2009, Norlights Press.

All of the above may be viewed on Amazon.com and other on-line booksellers. Author's web site: http://www.chargedbarticle.org/